Advertise!

An
Assessment of Fundamentals
for
Small Business

The author wishes to acknowledge
those who helped make, either directly or indirectly,
the completion of this book possible:

Mark A. Barbour
Jim Dixon
Ingrid Hubbard
Arnold L. Jack
Louise Ann Komives
Thomas D. Mack
D. Scott Miller
Charles Nabrit
Dan Poynter
Rini Ranbom
Rosemary Sova
Alan Stamper
Alan Vogt
Leanne R. Luscher
and
Thomas P. Luscher

for Mom

Advertise!
An Assessment of Fundamentals
for Small Business
by
Keith F. Luscher

Second Printing

published by:

K & L Publications
Post Office Box 09121
Columbus, Ohio 43209
SAN: 297-2484

Cataloging in Publication Data
Luscher, Keith F.
Advertise! An Assessment of Fundamentals for Small Business
by Keith F. Luscher
Includes Index
1. Advertising -- Self-promotion 2. Marketing -- Small Business
3. Graphic Design -- Production -- Handbooks, Manuals, etc. I. Title

Library of Congress Catalog Card Number:
90-91596

International Standard Book Number:
0-9625977-9-1

$14.95 Softcover

printed in
the United States of America

Advertise!

An
Assessment
of Fundamentals
for
Small Business

Keith F. Luscher

K&L
Publications

Columbus, Ohio

DISCARDED

IMPORTANT -- PLEASE READ

Table of Contents

Introduction

During my early years of college, I took a summer job with a small pizza shop in my hometown of Pittsburgh, Pennsylvania. While my job started out as a driver and pie-maker, I did get involved in organizing marketing strategies to boost the business of the store, which was only a few months old.

Since the business was new, there was not a big budget for promotions. One method the owner preferred was rounding up some of the local kids, taking them to some of the other areas to which we wished to expand, and having them go from house to house distributing flyer-coupons. The only payment those kids got was free pizza.

At a cost of barely seventy-five cents per pizza, one might assume it a highly economical promotion. But soon enough, the kids started asking *for more* than just pizza (could you blame them?).

So we sat down to make some decisions, and the budget made them for us. The only advertising which we could afford was in the classified ads.

We utilized a direct mail publication called *The Pennysaver*, and ran a 3 x 5 inch ad with coupons in it. The very day after that issue was mailed out, we had a surge of phone calls. In just one month, after some modest investments in the classifieds, we expanded our business threefold.

If you have purchased this book, I can only assume that you are interested in the many benefits which advertising and self-promotion have to offer. In researching the marketability of this product, I have seen many books on advertising, and the different aspects of it. There are separate books on marketing, copywriting, design, only a few which I could find on small space advertising, and several textbooks geared towards advertising students.

When most people think of advertising, they imagine multi-million dollar campaigns running on network television, and giant New York skyscrapers cutting up into the clouds. Not only is this the stereotype of the advertising profession, but it also tends to be the direction of the audience for many of the advertising books on the market.

You may consider advertising to be strictly a large financial expenditure, perhaps considerably more than your business can presently afford. You may think from what you have heard from others how advertising agencies may be out of your league simply because of your present lack of funds.

The truth is, you do not necessarily need an agency at first. *You* know your business better than anyone. That makes *you* one of the most qualified people to begin your own small scale ad campaign: a campaign which grows slowly, as your profits do. With just a few lines of type in the classified section of a newspaper or better yet, a national magazine, you can break into entirely new markets!

You may notice while reading this book that I refer to what you are selling to be the "product" This does not necessarily mean that it has to be a piece of merchandise off a shelf. A product can be anything: a service, a good, or even your entire business. When your whole business is the product being promoted in an ad, you're urging people to patron it.

Again, *you* are one of the most qualified people to lead up your ad campaign due to your knowledge and experience in your field of business. But you must also know some of the basics of advertising. That's where this book comes in.

In eight short chapters, the most essential points in the practice of advertising are made. Small space advertising is emphasized, because that is the best, and most economical area to break into. The chapters will not only inform, but they will *shape your attitudes.* This is what will give you a competitive edge, all the way from rough ideas in your head to finishing a black and white ad to be handed over to the publication.

As you apply the points described in this book, be patient. It will take practice to learn the field, and your first efforts may not be as successful as you may hope. If they don't, be sure not to make the same mistakes twice. Analyze what you did wrong, and what you can do to correct it.

As you read, you will find questions to ask yourself about your business. Get a notebook, and write these answers down as you get them. Have all your raw data collected together so that you can use it to formulate the most effective marketing strategy and promotions that you can.

Additional note from the author...

Since the information contained in this book may only be accurate up to the printing date, it is reasonable to assume that future, revised editions will be published. The author would appreciate any comments from readers on both the strengths and weaknesses of this book. Those comments which prove helpful are acknowledged, and those who submit them will receive a free copy of the Second Edition upon publication. Comments can be addressed to the author through the publisher.

Chapter

1

Advertising and Marketing

Before we examine the major points and benefits of advertising, we must first review another, strongly related concept: **marketing.** This is simply the process by which the exchange of goods occurs between the producer and the user for their mutual benefit.

In running a business, one of the first things that the manager must keep in mind is the **marketing concept**. As Lee Iacocca puts it: "Satisfy the customer." Only by doing this can a business truly be profitable. Make the products and provide the services at the convenience of the customer, and that customer will come back.

The "Marketing Mix"

In marketing a product, there are four main decisions which must be made first. They are:

1) What the Product Is. A product is a good or service which is bought and sold to gain some sort of satisfaction. The producer also decides what *attributes* the product will have (and which ones will be emphasized in selling it). These attributes can range from physical appearance to taste to basic consumer benefits (direct and indirect).

There are two types of products—**consumer goods** and **industrial goods**. Consumer goods are bought and sold to satisfy personal needs, industrial goods to satisfy business or industrial needs. If I run my own business, and I buy a computer to manage it, that's an industrial good. But if I buy a computer for my home to manage personal finances, then it's a consumer good. So you see, this definition lies not necessarily with the product itself, but with the *purpose it serves.*

Other classes of products include **specialty goods**, which are mainly luxury items of a specific brand. Examples include high-tech electronics, sports cars, designer clothes and gourmet foods. **Shopping goods** include some items which are specialties, but are not in such high demand, or sell on as much of an image as specialty goods do. Many products fall under both categories. Cars, clothes, appliances, and furniture, can be as expensive and inexpensive as we wish, depending on which particular items we select. We call most of them "needs" because they are basic items most of us are used to having around the house to make our lives a bit easier. Many of the products are still considered luxury, but not at the high price, prestige, or demand associated with specialty goods.

Finally, **convenience goods** are products purchased solely for purpose, not image or want. These include some grocery items, toiletries and utility products. For example, when was the last time you went into a drug store *just to browse,* as you may in a nice clothing or electronics store?

2) How Much It Will Cost. It is generally accepted that the more one product or brand costs over another, the better it is. Of course, the higher the quality, the higher it costs to produce. So, if an inferior product is overpriced, then chances are it won't sell.

3) How It Will Be Distributed. This is done mainly through the most common retailers utilized for the type of product. Mail order, however, is one of many marketing options available to the manufacturer.

4) How It Is Promoted. There are other methods of promotion, in addition to advertising. These methods are described in more detail in Chapter 6, which discusses public relations.

Market Defined

What is a market? When a product "hits the market," this generally means that it is made available to consumers in one way or another. When we hear the term **target market**, this refers to the group of people to which we believe our product will have some appeal.

The target market of auto makers and dealers can be just about the entire adult, working population. These markets must be broken down to **submarkets.** For instance, one may buy a new car anywhere from $5,000 to $200,000. Well, the people selling the more expensive automobiles will target the upper class citizens, while those selling less expensive cars will target middle to lower class citizens.

What Affects Marketing?

There are many uncontrollable conditions which determine how successful a product may be when it hits the market. They point out how unpredictable the business world can be, and that the "sure fire path to success" is a farce.

Some of the conditions affecting marketing are:

1) *Social and Cultural Attitudes.* Society has changed drastically over the last few decades. Women's roles have changed. Grocery shopping, once done mostly by women who were subsequently a prime target for advertising, is done by many men today. This has a drastic influence on how a product is to be marketed and how well it will sell.

2) *Economics.* The basic question of how much money people have to spend depends greatly on how well a product will sell. The best quality and priced product cannot sell if people don't have the money to buy it. As the economy and prosperity fluctuates, so does consumer spending.

3) *Technology.* The common record store may still be called that but today is selling fewer records than anything else. Why? Technology has yielded superior compact discs on the market, placing the record medium on borrowed time. You must examine the technological aspects of a potential product and make sure that it won't be obsolete in a few years. A major technological breakthrough can mean fortune for one, destitution for another.

4) *Consumer Preferences.* This element is most visible in "fads" which come and go. When entering a fad market, one must not waste time, because fancy watches which sell for $30 apiece today may be selling for 99 cents tomorrow.

5) *Demographics.* Demographics is the study of the data gathered on the distribution of people in accordance to age, sex, ethnic background, income, marital status, geographic location, and other aspects. The most accurate demographic statistics are developed every 10 years when the government conducts its census. This is important because if your target audience is not located within a specific area, it's foolish to advertise there.

For example, if you run a day-care service for children, you would not be wise to advertise your business in Sun City, Florida, where over 90 percent of the population is retired. Obviously, child care is of little concern to this segment of the population.

6) *Law and Politics.* If you are engaged in selling radar detectors or fireworks, you would not find much success (legally) in some states where those products are banned. In advertising, you must also be wary of how you might deliver some messages. If you feel uncertain about a market condition, your best bet is to seek legal advice before taking any action.

7) *Competition.* If yours is the only product of its type on the market, and is successful, it will not be alone for long. Products not only find competition with other brands of the same products, but also different products which serve the same purpose. While Coca-Cola and Pepsi battle it out, Seven-Up sells itself as the

"uncola," and a fruit juice distributor, Veryfine, successfully breaks into the soft drink market with classy ads and vending machines.

The Marketing Plan

Advertising is merely part of the whole **marketing plan**. When a business intends to promote a product or store, it sets **marketing objectives** for itself and lays out the plan to achieve them.

Marketing objectives always should be defined in quantitative terms (such as to increase sales of item x by 50 percent...) so success in achieving these goals can be measured. They also should be reasonably attainable, with a set time period over which the plan will be carried out.

In working with advertising either on your own, or with an agency, you must remember that advertising serves the goals of marketing. If the ad department is given a goal, it automatically becomes a marketing objective.

There are four elements which have an influence on the marketability of a product or business. Each affects the market in varying degrees. They are as follows:

1) *The Nature of the Market.* The type of people or organizations which are your target audience has a tremendous bearing on how you should promote yourself or your product. For example, a ritzy, expensive, men's cologne producer would be better off advertising in magazines like *GQ* or *Playboy* rather than *Boy's Life*,

simply because of the audiences to which these magazines are targeted.

2) *The Nature of the Product.* Whether your product is a consumer good or industrial good—it will still have to be promoted. However, as we stated before, promotions occur in various ways. You would not advertise industrial machinery the same way that you would advertise a new line of designer jeans.

3) *Life Span of the Product or Business.* Like humans, products and businesses tend to go through a life span or "cycle" as some refer to it. It begins at the **introductory stage,** when it is first introduced to the market. If the product type is new, promotion must work to stimulate **primary demand**, which is demand for the particular type of product. If this step succeeds, a stage of **vigorous growth** follows, while the product gains support and stability. If it is a really hot item, this is the point when the competitors will come out with all their imitations (remember the Sony Walkman, and all its imitations?) At this point, promotion must gear itself toward creating **selective demand**, or demand for a particular brand (namely, yours).

Next comes the **maturity level**, when the product or business holds its own profitably. This stage can last indefinitely, but most of the time, sooner or later, a stage of **decline** will occur. The producer then has two options: beef the product up with a new image, such as "improving" it or, pulling it from the market altogether. Let's look at an example mentioned previously. In the last six to seven years, record sales have steadily declined, primarily due to the development of compact discs. Obviously, the only choice is to pull them from the market (which the record companies have been gradually doing). There is one lesson to be learned: if you foresee your product or business eventually being wiped out by something obviously better, don't try to fight it...cut your losses and try to get in on the competition!

But what of the life span of a business itself? Up until about 20 years ago, most people would do their shopping at various small stores. There were (and still are...for now) fruit stands, butcher shops, fish markets, toy stores, hardware stores...a different store for each market. These businesses, especially the fruit stands and the butcher shops, are in steady decline due to the spread of enormous grocery and department stores, which combine all the products and services the smaller businesses have to offer.

4) *Financial Capabilities*. The last factor is basically how much money you are able and willing to spend on advertising. The amount of money spent varies widely, as does the selection in various media.

Other Things To Consider

Before getting too deep into a campaign or ad project to promote your business, you ought to consider the following questions:

1) *What are the basic attitudes of my customers towards what I'm selling?* If the attitudes are negative, you have a challenging task ahead of you. Perhaps the customers are not seeing a potential benefit that is clearly visible to you. Open their eyes! Illustrate that benefit; allow your customers to imagine themselves benefiting from your product.

2) *Who shops at my store?* If you operate a hardware store, most of the customers will probably be men, and so any advertising should be slightly geared towards them, but not too much! Remember, women shop in those places too. Also, remember that grocery shopping is conducted by just as many men as women. Don't make your customers feel stereotyped.

3) *What are potential turn-offs about my business?* What would turn you away? If you walked into a restaurant, and the look of the place gave you a sick feeling, would you feel like going there again, or even sticking around to eat now? Do you and your employees make your customers feel welcome, or are they given the feeling that they are an intrusion (while you may not give them that impression. Make sure that none of your employees do, either)?

4) *What products sell best?* Why do they sell? What qualities do they have, be them appearance or function, that slower selling products don't? How can you present these other products in a different light?

5) *What are my busiest days?* A good way to measure the success of promotion is to set a sale for a slower day, and see if business boosts. If you're advertising right in your store, do so on your busiest days.

Why Advertise?

There are reasons to advertise, and reasons not to. When a Midwestern construction company engaged in building condominiums in a town which had none, they relied on press releases for publicity rather than direct advertisements. Why? Because one of their marketing objectives was to build public support, and this was better achieved through independent press coverage (otherwise known as "publicity"-more on that in Chapter 6). Ads would have been considered "self-serving" by the public, not to mention more expensive.

When deciding whether or not to advertise, today's business owner must consider these questions:

1) Is *demand for my product, business or service rising?* This is crucial. Although some may feel otherwise, advertising cannot get people to buy what they didn't want in the first place. If I have a computer now, no ad, regardless of how clever, witty, funny, or tricky it may be, *will ever make me want to buy a typewriter.*

2) *Does our brand stand out from the rest?* Although some manufacturers do engage in advertising, the majority of dairy producers do not advertise their milk. That is left to their trade association. Why? Because most people generally feel that milk is milk, regardless of the brand. A product brand must have a uniqueness of some sort to stand out from the competition.

3) *What is its marketing appeal?* Appeal is a product's strongest selling point. In most cases, it is a benefit of some sort to the consumer. The benefit can be either direct or indirect. While one brand of toothpaste claims to give you a better checkup report when you go to the dentist, another promises to help you find a hot date for the weekend.

4) *Can we afford to advertise enough for it to be effective?* Although there are many ways to advertise

effectively without a heavy price tag (as you will find out later in this book), you must remember that in some cases, if you're not able to spend a certain amount, you're better off not spending any at all. Most third party presidential candidates do not advertise because they do not have the same funds to do so as the Republicans and the Democrats. They may have enough to buy some advertising, but in the end they're smart not to spend the few thousand dollars on what may become a hopeless cause.

If you really feel snagged on this question, your best bet may be to check with a consultant or ad agency.

5) *Does our product deliver what we say it should?* If it doesn't, word of mouth will defeat all that rented print and air time, and your product will fail.

What Advertising Sets Out to Do

Advertising has an ordered set of objectives. The first of these objectives is *to hook the attention* of the target audience. This is most important. The whole effort is in vain if this first goal isn't met. Once the attention is caught, the viewer's *interest must be stimulated.* A big heading might catch your eye, but unless you're encouraged to read or listen on, you will not *be informed* (the third goal) about the product. Once you have the information, you must be *motivated to act* on the impulses you are hopefully having to try the product. So, Remember these four points:

1) Hook
2) Interest
3) Inform
4) Motivate

Chapter 1

Types of Advertising

Retail Advertising is usually conducted locally. When you open a major metropolitan newspaper, and see full–page ads for sales in the local retail department store chain, this is retail advertising. They would not print the same ads in a national magazine, since their target audience is in the immediate area.

Mail-Order Advertising can be done on a local or national level. J.C. Penney does a fair share of business selling merchandise through their catalogues (which act as an ad medium). The customers shop at home by ordering over the phone, then receiving their merchandise through delivery or a catalogue center.

National Advertising occurs when a large manufacturer or nationwide chain of department stores advertises in national magazines and other publications, or on network television and radio.

Consumer Advertising is classified due not to its sponsor, but its audience. In this case, it is directed toward the general public, promoting normal consumer goods.

On the other hand, **Business Advertising** is directed towards the business community. A good example would be a company which makes copiers and business machines. While they are targeting the consumer group more and more, their primary target is still the business community.

Trade Advertising targets retailers and wholesalers who buy products and services to resell at a profit. Products would include practically anything tangible, while services would be insurance policies (to agents), travel packages, and food services.

Another form of business advertising, **Industrial Advertising**, promotes equipment, resources, and other things utilized by manufacturers in order to produce their products. Packaging and shipping is another example of what is traded through industrial advertising.

Professional Advertising is directed toward professional groups, such as the legal and medical professions. Members of these professions buy equipment and books. Architects and artists use art and drafting supplies. The manufacturers and dealers of these specialized goods are the sponsors of this form of advertising.

Public relations has a large hand in creating **Institutional Advertising**. This may not necessarily sell a product, but is used to generate public faith in the company or business itself. For instance, if a company makes a major decision, it may run ads explaining why and how that decision will benefit the consumer.

Public Service Advertising, which usually runs on donated space or air time, most often informs the public about a social issue or problem, offers advice, and is sponsored by companies in part to promote good public relations. An example would be when the manufacturers of alcoholic beverages run ads to discourage drinking and driving.

This chapter introduces the generally accepted practices and beliefs of the marketing and advertising profession. These are policies which are applicable to any business, regardless of size. To benefit the small business, the following chapters will discuss the opportunities available to them at an affordable level.

Chapter

2

The Advertising Media

The media are the ever-present entities which inevitably touch all our lives one way or another. This includes newspapers and television, radio and magazines. In fact, media possibly could not exist as we know it in this country without the presence of advertising.

THE MEDIA IN GENERAL

As stated above, mass media is in constant touch with us, regardless of our awareness. It is defined as that vehicle, be it television, newspaper, etc. which is designed for the very purpose of reaching the masses.

The two main forms of media are **print** and **broadcast**. The print media includes all newspapers and magazines. Of the newspapers, there are daily editions, weekly editions, and most metropolitan newspapers have large Sunday editions. One element of many Sunday editions which makes them unique from the rest are the magazine pull–out sections, featuring various special interest columns and colorful advertisements.

Perhaps magazines vary more than virtually all other forms of media. They are divided into three main groups: consumer, business, and farm publications.

Consumer magazines are the largest of the variety. They include general interest, which have a little bit of everything, and special interest, which can range from cars to interior decorating. These choices of topics exist in both national and regional publications.

The **business magazines** have a general area of interest also, but publishes magazines targeted at the industrial audience, offering titles such as *Appliance Manufacturer* to *Safety & Health.* Professional magazines such as *Medical World News* and the *ABA Journal* target the professions such as medicine and law.

General **trade publications** have perhaps one of the biggest varieties. They range anywhere from *Air-Line Pilot* to *Unfinished Furniture Magazine.*

Although the **farm magazines** are categorized separately, they are essentially the same as other trade magazines. They focus mostly on the business side of farming, with advice and articles on increasing profits, especially in these harder times. Even if a magazine or article focuses on crop growing techniques, the indirect goal for the farmer is to increase his profits.

Radio and television are the broadcast media. Television, in particular, has expanded greatly over the last 10 to 15 years, due to the advent of cable. Today, cable access broadens the prospect of advertising nationally without having to turn to the major networks. On top of that, there are now many special interest channels on the cable systems, as there are in magazines. The topics of these interests range from sports to health to science.

Selecting A Particular Medium

When selecting a medium, you must first decide how much you may want to spend. Obviously, you want to get the most out of your money, meaning you want your message to reach as many people as possible.

There is one important thing to consider here, though. As you may well be aware, the publications that have the widest readership are also the most expensive to advertise in. But the size of readership is not the only factor to consider. If I owned a computer store, and I wanted to expand my business nationwide through classified advertising in a national magazine, there are many publications which I could choose from.

Let's make up two fictitious magazines. One may be called *America*, a largely general interest magazine which publishes feature articles on the American scene. Another can be *Keyboard & Monitor*, a highly focalized publication for the computer industry. While both are national, *America* has a more diverse readership. Many of its readers may very well be interested in my business, but there is a sure bet that many of them won't. *Keyboard & Monitor*, on the other hand, has a readership of which almost all might be interested in my business.

A common method for comparing media charges is *the cost per thousand ratio* (**CPM**).

For the print media, the formula is:

CPM=	$\dfrac{\text{Cost of 1 B\&W Page Ad x 1000}}{\text{Publication's Circulation}}$

For the broadcast media:

CPM=	$\dfrac{\text{Cost of 1 unit of time x 1000}}{\text{Number of households reached at a certain time by a specific program}}$

The CPM need not be based on only the total circulation or households reached by a particular medium. If the correct demographic information is available, then a more accurate figure can be derived. For instance, let's say that I want to run a one-minute ad on the local television station during the evening news, and I know that the total number of households reached was around 150,000. Using the formula, and assuming that one minute of air time was $500, I could reach a CPM of about $3.30 per household.

But suppose that my ad is targeted to households with an income of over $80,000. Statistics tell me that out of those 150,000 households reached, roughly 70,000 fall under this category. Now in order to achieve a more accurate CPM, I merely replace the figure of 150,000 with 70,000, giving me a figure of around $7.15 per household (in my target).

Now you may wonder what difference it makes, since I'm paying the same lump sum, anyway. Well, suppose I want to run that ad for the computer program again. My two options (of course, the options are usually much more than two) are again *America* and

Keyboard & Monitor. My target audiences are adults who are seriously interested in computing. Let's say that *America's* total circulation is around 800,000, and *Keyboard & Monitor's* is about 500,000. If demographic studies tell me that about one fourth of *America's* total audience falls under my target category, while nearly all of *Keyboard & Monitor's* does, which magazine is the better advertising choice?

What Media for What Market?

The next question you must ask yourself is, *what media would be most suitable for my purpose?* Your purpose will tell you how selective you may want to be in choosing your audience. The less selective, the wider audience you can target your product to, and the more versatile your advertising approach can be.

Suppose you own an auto parts store. Your main audience would be males, anywhere from their late teens to past retirement age. Let's say that your business is strictly local. What media would be best for you? Well, you would want to place your spot where you would be confident that this group would see it. If using the broadcast media, a good spot would be during a sports event, or a TV show targeted mainly at the male audience. If you choose to use the print media (probably your best buy), the newspaper and local publications would be the best choice. Many cities have small publications strictly for the purpose of advertising for cars and accessories. Some national publications (not only for cars) publish locally, meaning that the issues vary slightly from area to area (much like *TV Guide* does). This process of advertising on a strictly local basis is called **geographic selectivity**.

Just How Can We Tell How Many People Will See Your Ad?

This depends on how big a medium's audience is. The media themselves can tell you their circulations and ratings as verified by independent auditing organizations.

Characteristics of Different Media

Some media have a greater command of audience attitudes and respect than others. Long-time newspaper columnists tend to collect followings as do TV and radio personalities. With images and personalities, a certain level of prestige and authority develops. If your ad is placed among this sort of media company, it can do wonders for the impact of your message.

Another diverse set of characteristics to be considered is that of **flexibility** and **frequency**. These are two main advantages that the broadcast media have over the print media. In radio and TV, you can have your ad to the public within hours and as often as you can afford. This tends to make the business rule of expecting the unexpected easier to adhere to. If you suddenly find yourself overstocked with certain items and need to get rid of them in a short period of time (obviously at good prices), you can make this message known to the public with as little as a telephone call.

The print media are not so flexible, nor as frequent. Newspapers are about the most flexible of the print media, simply because they publish most often. Rarely can even newspapers grant same day service. Most ads can't be run for at least 24 hours. Magazines take even longer. Most ads must be placed more than a month in advance, and can be seen only as often as the publication is printed, which can be from weekly to yearly (with the vast majority being monthly).

The question of **durability** then comes up. This is defined as the potential for an ad to be seen more than once by the same person. It can be done in the broadcast media but only at a high expense. You are paying through the nose *each time* your ad is merely seen, even out of the corner of one's eye. Have you ever been interested in a product in a TV ad which merely caught your attention for a fleeting second, only to be frustrated that you didn't catch that toll-free number or address to place the order, or the store where it could be found? Have you ever felt like waiting to see if they would run that ad again before the show was over?

Now just imagine if you were flipping casually through a magazine, or paging through a newspaper, and the same product caught your eye. Now what do you do? Just turn back a few pages and there it is. The product, the pitch, the benefits, and most importantly, *how to get it.*

Media Combinations

Another question to be asked in reaching as many prospective customers as possible is what sort of media combination, if any, should you use? You must consider the pluses and minuses of each category: newspaper, magazines radio and television, much of which have already been described, and will be further explored as we continue.

Here is a good place to explain one definition: **waste**. Remember that in advertising, waste is defined *as playing your message to someone who is not in the position to be able or inclined to buy.* (You don't promote feminine hygiene products to men.) Of course this is a goal that is never fully achieved, but you always work towards it.   The degree of waste expected must be considered when selecting a medium or a mixture of them.

But why would you want a mixture at all? Perhaps you would want to utilize the different advantages which the print and broadcast have to offer. We know that to provide the durability that is more common with print would be very expensive in broadcast. But who ever said that the messages would have to be exactly the same? A radio or television ad could deliver a very broad, "catch your interest" ad, then provide information on how to obtain more information. Have you ever heard the expression on TV commercials, "See our ad in this Sunday's paper..."? Or how about a print ad with that ever present little TV square which reads, "As seen on TV"? These sort of strategies in mixing media make the most out of your advertising dollar.

Broadcast Media: Radio

Of the two broadcast media, radio is the oldest. Though it once had the status which television holds today, there were many who believed that the advent of television would bring the death of radio. Obviously they were wrong. Radio has with time found its own place among the media, and it even has times of the day when it outrates television!

With more than five hundred million radios, and more than eight thousand radio stations in the United

States today, one can hardly say that it isn't a medium worth looking at.

Radio is one of the best, and most economical ways to reach a target audience. The appearance of TV caused many changes in radio in the fifties, requiring different radio stations to focus on different audiences by offering diverse tastes in music and other programming.

In meeting one of the standards explained previously, radio is a medium of very high frequency. I'm not referring to the technical aspect, but rather how often your ad may be run in a given period of time. The cost is, of course, much less than television, and ads cost less individually when bought in "bulk" packages.

Referring to the previous section on media combinations, radio often supplements a major advertising investment in an alternate medium. Brief radio spots can reinforce other messages, deliver their own about your product, and even advertise your other advertisements.

Radio also offers a wide range of selectivity. Radio's most highly rated hours, when it actually does outrate TV, are during the morning and evening rush hours, otherwise known as the drive times. These are the best (and most expensive) times to nail the target audience of the daily work force. The domestic audience (the homemakers and the shoppers) are then the primary targets of the hours falling between the "big commutes." It is generally recognized that the most common place people listen to the radio is in their cars.

Another advantage of radio advertising is the low

cost of producing the commercials. An advertiser can produce several variations of the same ad in one recording session. The flexibility in scheduling also allows the advertiser to choose which ads will run, and when.

Some disadvantages of radio do exist, of which the advertiser must be aware. Although radio is good for reaching a target audience, it is generally not as effective for reaching the mass audience. To do this, you would have to run your ads on various types of stations, which would subsequently run up your advertising bill.

Another thing to consider is, since radio is strictly audio, your product cannot be visualized as it can in print, or demonstrated as it can on television.

If you turn to an ad agency (more on these in Chapter Eight), you may find that many of them are more reluctant to give their best effort to radio campaigns, due to the lack of commissions it gives them. Many larger radio stations may indeed have advertising people on their staff, if your need is to simply run a single radio spot.

The term "spot" refers to spot radio. Spot radio differs from network radio in that it is cheaper and easier to produce, because it is contracted on a local basis, for single station use. Its advantages are much of what was just discussed, working locally with a much more defined audience.

Network radio is a chain of radio stations sharing the same transmissions, much like television. The various radio networks include the "Big Three," ABC,

NBC and CBS, in addition to the Mutual Broadcasting System, and various smaller groups. Stations affiliated with these networks enjoy many benefits similar to TV stations. In addition, some radio networks are not national like the TV networks. Some may only reach a group of states, serving their geographic purpose.

Like papers and magazines, radio also has a **circulation**. This is defined by the number of households which tune in to that particular station. **Coverage** is determined by the strength and height of the station's transmitter, its location and terrain features.

It is at this point where we reach another formula for determining your advertising dollar's worth. What we have now are gross rating points (or **GRP**'s).

> 1 GRP = 1% of total potential audience

One point is equal to one percent of the total radio (or television) audience in a specific area. So, if a certain rock concert broadcast were heard by 15 percent of the total audience, then that program (and the commercials aired during it) would have 15 GRP's. The GRP's are added each time the commercial is broadcast, depending on the point rating of the program it is sponsoring. Suppose I have a commercial that I want aired twice in one week, during two different programs. If one program has a rating of 15 GRP's and the other has a rating of 17, then my commercial's total GRP rating for that week would be 32.

Broadcast Media: Television

As you may know, television is the most expensive medium in use in advertising. It has a wide range of advantages and disadvantages. Overall, it is known for its ability to give a powerful impact, swaying people to take action. This is primarily because of its visual capabilities. Television commands much more attention than radio.

Television usually gets most of the viewers' attention and keeps it. It has the ability to demonstrate the product it is promoting, and the more talented the people creating these visual messages, usually the more intense the messages become.

Many of the terms for describing the TV audience are the same as those of radio. **Coverage** and **circulation** as in radio, describe respectively, the number of homes receiving the signal and those tuning into it. Coverage of cable television depends on the number of the subscribers.

As with radio, the size of a station's or network's audience depends greatly on the time of day. The most popular and expensive viewing time is, as you may know, *prime time*—which starts at 7:30 p.m. and ends at 11 p.m., seven days a week. The next most popular time is 4:30 to 7:30 p.m., also seven days a week. The average household is said to watch more than 48 hours (two days worth!) of TV a week, with this figure climbing as the number of people and TV's in each household rises.

Most television stations have a wider target audience than do radio stations. They tend to play a greater variety of programming. These types of programs range from adventures and dramas to sitcoms. Typically, the more ratings one program gets on one station, usually the lower the ratings for another program on another station at the same time. Although there is an extremely large portion of audience to attract, each program usually only attracts a small percentage of it.

Since the overall audience is so large, if we break down the costs via the CPM formula we find that, per person, *television is actually less expensive.* This is because the difference in advertising costs between TV and other media *is actually smaller than the difference in total viewing audiences of each medium.* If TV gets three times the audience of radio, yet only costs twice as much, you're getting more for your money.

Network Advertising

Network advertising is probably the most prestigious of all. One difference between radio and television is that nearly all of the prime time programming on television is run by the network (with the exception of independent stations, though even these have decreased with the birth of the FOX network). Another difference is that the ad slots are carefully sorted out, and there are only so many to go around. After all, a network can only run one ad at a time.

Because few advertisers can afford to be the sole sponsor of a network prime time program, we now have what are called **participations**. Participations occur when advertisers group together, each buying segmented time slots (or units), each lasting about 30 to 60 seconds (with most lasting about 30 seconds) which are run back to back during each commercial break.

Networks do take breaks between programs allowing for affiliates to provide local advertising and station identification. These slots are known as **adjacencies.**

Spot Television is advertising to a local audience, through a local station. While less expensive than the networks, the costs vary according to the individual stations requirements.

The broadcast day is divided into three parts: *daytime, prime time,* and *late night.* Prime time is so called due to its heavy audience. A 30- second spot can cost anywhere from $50,000 to $150,000. Daytime, which runs from 7 a.m. to 4:30 p.m., is the cheapest. Thirty-second spots here start at around $10,000. Late night, which is dominated by talk shows and movies, sells 30 second spots for about $15,000 to $20,000.

During prime time, networks are allowed to sell up to 9 minutes of each hour to commercial time. Independent stations can sell up to 12 minutes for each hour. During the day and at late night, all stations can sell up to 16 minutes for each hour.

The Print Media: Consumer Magazines

In order to evaluate the advertising worth of the 1,200 consumer magazines currently on the stands today, we must first divide them into categories defining their basic audience appeal. These periodicals come out at varying intervals, ranging from annually to quarterly to bimonthly, with most being monthly and weekly. Most are available by subscription and over the newsstand counter. A few are available through only one of these channels.

All consumer magazines are divided first into

general interest and special interest magazines. Examples of **general interest magazines** would be *The Saturday Evening Post* and *The New Yorker.* These publications carry articles of interest to everyone. **Special interest magazines**, such as *Video Review* and *Sports Illustrated*, have been on the steady rise, and are outnumbering the general interest publications rapidly. Obviously, they are aimed at groups with specific interests. Today, virtually every hobby and interest has a magazine which accompanies it. Among the most popular groups of special interests are publications aimed at women and car buffs. These groups are divided even more. Women's groups are divided distinctly, with publications like *Seventeen* for the adolescent and *Cosmopolitan* for the adult population.

One of the best advantages of magazines over all the other media is that they can last for a long time. People do not throw out magazines as they would newspapers. They lie around for months, even years. Doctors' offices and waiting rooms usually have magazines pile up for months. Just imagine the numbers and the variety of people who sit there for hours every day just paging through. A single ad in a single magazine can convey its message to literally hundreds of people, or more!

Another plus is that in print, the reproduction is more colorful, and there is more thought generally given to magazine ads over newspaper ads. There is also much greater flexibility in both design and layout. The design can be a fold-out, pop-up, or practically anything that the advertiser is willing to pay for. When Camel cigarettes celebrated its 100th birthday, it printed ads which had little musical devices singing "Happy Birthday". A well-known condom manufacturer placed an ad in *Playboy* with a free condom sample in it (although dealers had to battle to keep people from coming in and stealing the condoms without buying the magazines).

Probably the best advantage that special interest publications offer is the selectivity. Most products are made for specific groups of people, and these publications provide direct access to those groups. The wider the groups, the more magazines you can choose to advertise in without having waste.

Since most consumer magazines are distributed nationally, they can provide an immediate national exposure. Plus the loyal readers of these magazines, of which there are usually many, look to these publications with trust and confidence. Many of the readers spend a lot of time just looking at the ads.

Since advertising costs per magazine are based on circulation, most magazines charge a fee based on what is called a **rate base**. This is the *guaranteed minimum circulation* for each month. Although the circulation of a particular month may increase a bit, if it decreases below the rate base, the advertisers receive a rebate on their investment.

The available spaces of ads are based on the size of the magazine itself. Most magazine sizes are around 8-1/2 x 11 inches, with a page size (area of printing) at around 7 by 10 inches. An advertiser may purchase portions of these full pages.

If your business is aimed at the local market, you may still print ads in local editions of national magazines. *TV Guide* is a prime example. It prints locally, so many of the ads in the Pittsburgh edition will differ from the Columbus edition, though both may be issued the same week.

The Print Media: Newspapers

For the small business wanting to get exposure in the local market, newspapers are a remarkable and economical medium. They are highly regional, and many have extremely wide circulations. Also, each newspaper is usually read by an average of two to three people. Even large national distributors will utilize them when breaking into regional markets.

Even more so in the newspaper than the magazine ads can range from sizes of about an inch width to several pages. There is literally no limit to the size, providing the advertiser has the money to pay for it. Newspapers reach wide varieties of audiences. Suffice it to say that they are general interest publications, but each issue is usually divided into fields of more focused interests like sports, finance, food, arts and other departments. This allows the advertiser to choose the audience to be targeted.

If you made a phone call right now you could have an ad in tomorrow morning's edition. This is one of the best advantages newspaper advertising has to offer. If you see a great marketing opportunity arise suddenly, or if you want to get a head start on a competitor, in many cases, that step is taken with a phone call to a newspaper. Plus, your ad can be in every issue, every day if you like. And you would be surprised at how affordable it can be.

Of course, there are disadvantages as well. As

stated before of magazines, readers usually throw out newspapers after a day or so. No one wants to read an old newspaper. So, after a short run the paper is in the garbage or at the bottom of a bird cage, where it is unlikely to be read and in any event will be quickly obliterated.

There are many types of newspapers in print today. First are the **daily newspapers**, which come out at least once, and usually twice, a day. More than 75 percent of the dailies across the country publish morning and evening editions. It is believed that the evening edition enjoys the most reading, since the morning and afternoon ones come out in the midst of the average day's hustle and bustle.

Small towns and suburbs are the most common places to find **weekly newspapers** in America today. Right now there are almost 8,000 weeklies in circulation, and they are steadily growing. The goal of the weeklies is not to compete with the big metropolitan newspapers, but rather to emphasize purely local news. Since the news is strictly local, usually so is the advertising. This provides an excellent opportunity for businesses to make their messages known in the area. Another aspect unique to weeklies is that they are not usually discarded so quickly, as the readers will have to wait another week for the release of the next edition.

Sunday newspapers, which are usually large editions of papers which publish during the week as well, have the greatest circulation. They may have a circulation of 20 to 40 percent above the daily editions. This means a much larger volume of advertising.

The Sunday paper has something of interest to just about everybody, even younger readers. Of all the departments and sections the dailies have to offer, the Sunday papers usually offer more in each section. So, if you run a furniture or electronics store, you can advertise in the "home" section. If you sell toys, advertise in the comics (although this practice is on the decline since it was revealed that most of the readers of comics are adults, not children), and so on.

The Sunday supplement is a magazine (usually with color) of some sort, resembling a consumer magazine, although people tend to give it the same life span as the rest of the paper. Another similarity between the Sunday supplement and the consumer magazine is that the supplement usually has longer closing dates than the rest of the paper. However, unlike consumers, it is usually in the trash by the end of the next day. Two of the major Sunday supplements are *Parade* and *Family Weekly*. They are produced nationally and sold to individual papers, each having its heading at the top of the cover page.

As you move on, you will learn more about other advertising media and the benefits of small space advertising. Small space advertising offers an excellent opportunity to build or expand your business slowly, investing more as you earn more.

Chapter 3

Non-media Advertising

Non-media advertising uses methods other than print or broadcast to promote a product or business. Major uses in non-media advertising include direct mail advertising (not to be confused with mail-order), outdoor advertising, and transit advertising.

Direct Mail Advertising

Direct mail is one of the largest forms of direct response marketing, in terms of how much is spent on it. Nearly $16 billion is spent on direct mail every year. At one time, what was once referred to as "junk mail" (unaddressed sales pieces which would stuff people's mailboxes full), gave this medium a shaky reputation. Now, with government legislation to control the overflow by requiring most direct mail advertising be addressed, it can bring you worthwhile coupons and sale items, many of which come in packs together issued by cooperative direct mail agencies. The advertisers in the **co-ops** pay a fee for the circulated ads.

There are many advantages to direct mail advertising. One of these is **selectivity**, which is being able to *choose* who will see your ads. A topic we discussed previously is waste, which, again, is defined as delivering your message to those who are not potential buyers. Well, with direct mail, you have greater selectivity, thus reducing your waste. The ads can be distributed by targeted markets, including neighborhoods, entire zip codes, cities, or by the individual. There are countless ways to select your potential buyers. Usually the names are taken from resident mailing lists.

Another advantage is **impact**. When your potential customer receives your message in the mail, there is little else for it to compete with. Direct mail ads can be addressed to either person by name, or by the term, "occupant." When addressing someone by name, consider how important it may be to do so, depending on what it is you're advertising. Remember that as much as 25% of the names on most mailing lists are inaccurate. If you are simply trying to reach a mass audience, then you're best to leave the names off.

Business reply envelopes and other convenient reply methods for the consumer will increase your response as well, if a mail-back reply is needed. If one must go to the trouble of preparing and stamping an envelope, you are much less likely to receive a response than if a self–addressed, stamped or metered envelope or post card is included in the mailing. Some direct mail advertisers will even print addressee's names on removable, self adhesive labels that can be affixed to a post card and simply dropped in the mail in order to increase responses.

Direct mail can generate responses which are highly measurable. Since the promotion is usually made through only one channel, and the response is the same, it is quite easy to count how many responses come in for how many mailings sent out. You are also able to keep track of the geographic areas and types of customers which generated the most responses.

Mailing Lists

As mentioned before, the addresses are usually generated from resident and other companies' mailing lists. This is one of the most important factors of direct mail advertising. These mailing lists are acquired from what are called **list managers**. These individuals provide mailing lists for a percentage of the revenues received (around 15%) through responses. Many of these managers work for magazines or other larger mail–order businesses.

Another source of mailing lists is the **list broker**. List brokers are usually able to provide more special-ized mailing lists which are directed towards particular types of consumers. He or she may be another advertiser or simply an individual who compiles lists and rents them to others. The variety of lists is usually greater, ranging from very generalized to very specialized. The more specialized a list is, the more expensive it is likely to be.

One thing to remember is that often, but not always, lists are not given to the company itself, but rather to the party which does the mailing (in many cases, a printer of some sort). The advertiser renting the list only sees the names of the respondents.

There are two forms of mailing lists: compiled and mail–derived. **Compiled lists** are usually assembled by brokers who rent lists from other publications and advertisers. The lists are then as specialized as the broker wants them to be. They can be from people who joined record clubs in the last year to those who spent over $500 on a single mail–order item. One thing to remember: the older a list is, the less reliable it is likely to be.

Mail-derived lists are usually much more efficient. They are strictly made up of those customers who have ordered by mail in the past from one or more companies. It can be a house list, or made up yourself from your own past customers or those another advertiser who may share the same interests.

As you might have guessed, the renting and selling of mailing lists is, in itself, a big business.

Other forms of direct mail advertising are through **package inserts**. This consists of the other pamphlets stuffed in your utility bills every month, or other products or items you might get in the mail on a regular basis. This is economical for both the advertiser and the issuer of the mailed item because it allows them to split the mailing costs, and gives them a wide circulation.

The envelopes stuffed with various forms of coupons are examples of **co-op mail advertising**. This is another method of reducing costs. Another benefit is that people are more apt to pay attention to a packet filled with "great bargains" (as it is usually described on the outside), and go through them, paying attention to every detail, whereas solo mailings or solo inserts may be quickly discarded without a glance.

If marketing a product or service which requires a direct reply, it may be beneficial to select lists of people who have previously ordered products related to or similar to yours.

Planning a Direct Mail Campaign

Most business which advertise through direct mail are involved in other forms of marketing as well. These businesses may also be involved in advertising in the media, therefore intensifying the campaign.

There are many forms of direct mail advertising. They can range from sales offers made in envelope packets (with brochures cover letters, and convenient means of response), simple pamphlets in the mail, or mere postcards. Obviously, the more elaborate, the more expensive to produce and to mail.

The three types of paper stocks used in direct mail are **writing stocks, book stocks,** and **cover stocks.**

Writing stock is any paper that is written or typed on. This is used most often for stationery, and should be used for cover letters for packets.

Cover stocks are the strongest and toughest. They are not only used as covers to books, but as postcards and pamphlets. They can be either glossy or rough on the surface, with one side usually being glossy.

Figure 3-1. Above is an example of a direct mail piece, stuffed in an envelope with others just like it (ad courtesy of Val-Pak).

Book stocks have a great variety. The most commonly used is the **machine finish** paper. It is relatively tough, and easy to print on. Another commonly used type of book stock is **newsprint**. It is the least expensive, and the cheapest in quality as well. Most things printed on this type stock are not intended to be kept for long periods. Newspapers and some magazines utilize this inexpensive resource.

Printers come with all sorts of differing capabilities and rates. The selection of a printer should not be made hastily. Get plenty of estimates. If it is out of town, that's fine, but be sure that it is the right choice for you.

If you own a business which markets a variety of merchandise (although it may be geared to a specific audience), you may want to consider starting up a catalogue service. This project may not be as expensive as it sounds. An initial black and white publication may cost well under a dollar a copy if the correct resources are utilized. **This method of direct marketing can very well double your business—or more.**

Outdoor Advertising

As you may have guessed, outdoor advertising consists of the billboards not only along our nation's roads and highways, but also on the sides of buses and other transit vehicles. Other forms of outdoor advertising are posters and circulars which are displayed outside.

There are many things to think about when considering outdoor advertising. It has its advantages and disadvantages. Because outdoor displays are very inexpensive the demand is great, you may have to wait months to years for a specific sign to become available.

Unlike direct mail, outdoor advertising is not very selective, which makes it a good choice for those trying to reach a wide variety of audiences. Moreover, you can only say so much on a giant billboard or bus panel, which may only be seen for an average of just a few seconds; therefore, using outdoor signs with only a few words and a single, large image can be very helpful in cuing the audience to remember another ad of yours which they may have seen in a magazine or on television.

Like direct mail, outdoor advertising has suffered from a bad reputation as well. At one time, billboards were reaching the point where they were becoming an eyesore. Public interest groups and environmentalists lobbied to maintain control over the flood of outdoor advertising, leading to the Highway Beautification Act of 1965.

This form of non-media advertising has been a great resource to the tobacco industry, which is forbid-

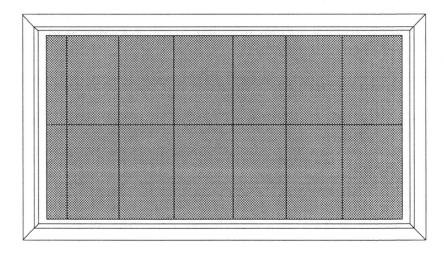

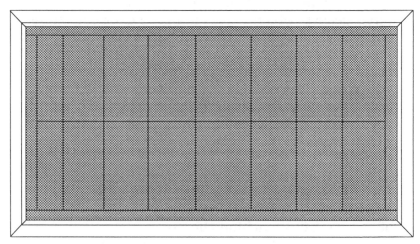

Figure 3-2. *Diagrams of both 30 Sheet (top) and Bleed Poster (bottom) billboards.*

den from advertising on television. The advertisement of such products which hold a negative connotation in many peoples' minds may have been a contributing factor to the negative reputation of outdoor advertising, which is gradually abating.

Upon deciding to utilize outdoor advertising, you must decide exactly where you want your message to be displayed. You would consider the same demographic information as in other campaigns. When you have done this, find out who the local outdoor plant operator is. They will arrange the lease and fee arrangements. If a board must be built first, then they will do so (all involved parties permitting). They should also maintain the condition of the sign while the lease is active.

The design for these boards can be done by the contractors, but at an increased expense. Once your sign is up, you are the best person to conduct your inspection as well.

The most common form of billboard display is the **poster panel.** This panel is made to hold the entire image by a series of connecting posters which are pasted to the billboard. They can be purchased or rented in virtually any quantity, with a minimum lease period of about 30 days, and may be either illuminated or nonilluminated boards. Illuminated boards cost more and are located where traffic is most active all hours of the day. They are also available in either **30-sheet** and **bleed poster** sizes, each of which has an average size of around 12 by 25 feet. On bleed posters, the image (i.e., the printed area) meets the edge of the board, whereas the 30-sheet does not. Rather, the 30–sheet has a blank (usually white) border lying between the image and the frame of the billboard (see Fig. 3-2).

Another type of poster, most commonly used in the city is the **junior poster**, or the "eight sheet poster." This board is about 5 by 11 feet, and is much more popular in the city due to regulations and available space.

The rates at which billboards are rented are determined by the gross rating point basis (GRP). Depending on its size and location, each board has a GRP rating of 100, 75, 50, or 25. In other words, a board with a rating of 50 GRP's will give exposure to an audience equal to 50 percent of the total potential market.

Let's take a city with a population of one million, and your target audience is that of women between the ages of 18 and 45. If about 30% of the total population fits this category, then that would give you a potential market of about 300,000 people. If you were to rent a board which had a rating of 50 GRP's, then your market exposure would be around 150,000 people (50% of 300,000).

Local reports on the exposure of outdoor ads are conducted by an independent organization known as Audience Measurement by Market of Outdoor (AMMO). This organization conducts surveys of people's recollections of outdoor ads the results of which, after factoring in appropriate demographic information such as frequency of travel, are then translated into GRP's.

Besides the conventional poster boards, there are two other forms of outdoor advertising. **Painted bulletins** are billboards on which the advertising is painted, rather than made up of connecting printed posters pasted to the board. They are much more expensive and permanent. They are only considered for areas of extremely high traffic.

The other form is what is a **spectacular**. This is an outdoor sign with all the fixins'. It is specifically designed and built to the specifications of the advertiser. An example of this would be those seen in big cities (especially in the East) which advertise a coffee, or a soft drink. There is usually a mechanical device which gives the illusion of the product pouring into a cup or a glass of some sort. Another example would be that immense Coca-Cola sign made completely of colored lights in Times Square in New York City. Spectaculars are the most expensive form of outdoor advertising and should be considered only when setting up on a permanent basis.

Overall, when considering an outdoor location, there are a few things you must consider. The first is whether the location and sign being put up is attractive. The last thing you want is something that looks ugly or pathetic.

The second is, look around and see if there are any other features which may distract people from it. When people drive by the site, you want them to remember *your* sign, not the spectacular sitting right next to it.

Also, make sure that it is on a relatively long stretch of road, so that people will see it from afar. If it's posted around a sharp curve, a driver will have to go by five to ten times to finally grasp the message.

Be sure to check that no trees or other natural or man-made structures will be blocking it.

Finally, after considering these things, ask yourself: Is it worth the price?

One of the most important questions is that of aesthetic value. The more attractive and creative it is, the better it gets the job done. Images and words should go together. Capital letters should be used as little as possible, due to their blocky shape. They are much more difficult to read from afar than small letters.

Transit Advertising

One of the fastest growing types of advertising is that of **transit advertising**. This consists of the ads you see on and in buses, subways, taxis, in train and bus stations, airports, and even on benches at bus stops. There are three categories of transit advertising: **station advertising, interior advertising** and **exterior advertising.** Buses and trolleys are the most frequently used medium for this type of advertising, and they use virtually all three categories. There are ads on the outside of the buses and trolleys, ads on the inside, and ads where you get on and off.

Interior Transit Advertising

This form has expanded rapidly due to the growth of mass transit systems. A variety of people use these systems frequently, and they're good for opening up to a wide exposure for a modest price. Most advertisers seeking out a less selective audience are advised to consider what it has to offer.

Most interior advertising consists of what we call **car cards**. These are cards you see on a bus, trolley, subway or train above the heads of people sitting across from you. They come in various sizes, and are relatively inexpensive to produce.

The common method of rating the efficiency of interior transit advertising is by use of **service values**. The coverage of the market, be it 100, 75, 50 or 25 percent, depends on the number of car cards an advertiser decides to utilize. The more cards, the greater the cost. Sizes of the cards, of which there are many, also affects cost. The summary of the costs for them can be found on the **rate card**, which is compiled by the transit organization.

Exterior Transit Advertising

The most common form of **transit advertising** is that found on buses. They are literally what you might call "mobile billboards", and can thus reach an even wider variety and number of people (when the sides of the buses aren't covered with dirt or the sign isn't upside down—not an uncommon trait with some bus lines).

Exterior ads on buses come in various sizes. Three sizes for the sides of the bus, and two smaller sizes, one for the front and another for the rear of the bus. Like interior ads, they are sold based on the number of displays. Each bus line has different routes and varying exposure. If you wish to achieve a certain showing (or GRP), they will know the amount of ads required to achieve the desired level.

Figure 3-3. An example of station advertising.

Station Advertising

Station advertising is seen in many different locations. They are not only in bus stations and airports, but in malls, lobbies and other businesses. The quality of each differs with the location in which it is seen.

Most station advertising is done by posters. Although they can contain a bit more information than billboards, they must have an eye catching quality to get passers-by to stop and read them. How the posters are displayed depends on the location. Regular bus stations may have display cases, while some subway stations may just use paste. Airports frequently have stylish illuminated cases, which allow them to blend in to attractive surroundings.

Most display advertising and outdoor ads provide a great supplement to campaigns conducted in different media. The images are usually seen for less than a few seconds, but it does offer a great potential to get a wide coverage at a modest price. If you run a small business or restaurant near a highway, outdoor advertising is something to be considered if you have not already done so. Since it is given the least amount of scrutiny, it is the most visual medium. There is no question of the rate of its growth. We can only hope that our society does not become too flooded, not only for environmental reasons, but because over-saturation would almost certainly cause the ads to lose their effectiveness.

Chapter 4

Small-Space Advertising

Small space advertising, mainly seen in the classified sections of newspapers and magazines, is an inexpensive and highly efficient way to begin your advertising campaign.

Your first impression may be that it would not be as efficient, but think again.

When you look through the classified section of a newspaper or magazine, ask yourself the following question: *"Why am I doing this?"*

Why are you doing this? There aren't any pictures or articles to read. There isn't anything other than advertisements to interest the reader.

So why is the reader looking through the classifieds? Why are the classified sections of both newspapers and magazines divided into sections, such as for "Help Wanted", "Services Offered", "For Sale", etc.? Why not throw them all into one big pile?

People do not page through these sections to be entertained. They are there because they have some basic interest in what the advertisers have to offer. They may not be looking for anything specific, but they generally feel that they will know it when they see it.

When you advertise in the classifieds, there is very little chance of having waste (remember, waste is exposing your ad to someone who is *not* a potential buyer). ***Remember this: Everyone who looks through the classifieds is a potential buyer, or else they wouldn't be there in the first place.***

If you look through the classifieds, be it newspaper or magazine, you may see that not all the advertisers are small businesses or mail-order outfits. Large companies and corporations still use them when breaking into a new market or looking for employees.

Who Can Use the Classifieds?

Before going into how to prepare a classified advertisement, which still must be worded very carefully, you may wonder what the classifieds can do for your business.

Small businesses exist in a great variety. Some are more unique than others. Whether you market goods or services, you can still use the classifieds.

If you run a service, obviously the best thing to do is advertise in the local papers. Your phone number is one channel through which your responses will come.

But suppose you're a retailer of some sort. Are there products of which you have too large a stock? Have you ever considered moving to another area where you feel that it would be more profitable, only to be held back by the heavy costs of the move?

Classified advertising not only can make the benefits your business has to offer more widely known in your town or city, but known across the nation, and by the exact people who would be interested in your products.

Suppose I own a small comic book/collectible merchant store. I make a living from many of the people who share an interest in the merchandise I sell: comic books, paperbacks, records, collectible toys and models, some antiques, posters, etc. I buy as well as sell. But the number of potential customers in my area are limited. Therefore, my business is limited by geography.

Then I stumble onto the benefits of classified advertising. This could be a way to not only increase sales, but to expand my inventory. If I've been getting a flow of inquiries (which means an accelerated demand) about a particular series of comic books, of which my supply is low, I can make it known through the classifieds that I am interested in buying these comic books from whoever is willing to part with them.

Now let's take another example. Suppose I have not seen much of a local demand for this particular product, of which I then have many. How do I get rid of them? I could run ads for it in any of the many magazines which are targeted toward my market (and which I would probably sell in my store), such as *Starlog* and *Fangoria.* Instantly, my business would be made visible to people *nationwide.* Now, I have two choices. I can either advertise my product, or advertise my business. My business could be advertised by way of offering a free catalogue (which would not cost much to have printed—well under a dollar a copy) which has my entire inventory. It could be updated every six months. Although this may not create an instant financial turnover, if strategically planned I could surely see an increase in sales.

Almost any product can be sold through **direct marketing**, which is selling through the mail. The trick is in the advertising.

Creating Your Classified Ad

Classified ads are easy to write. Since it is pure copy, with little or no design or illustration (although larger **display ads** may include one or both of these elements), it can be drafted up on a single sheet of paper in a matter of minutes. You can even read it directly to the publication over the phone.

Most classified ads don't exceed 20 words. How many words you may want would depend on your message.

Your ad will be placed in the proper category of the publication (heeding the information from the previous chapters). At this point, you must determine what it will take to get your readers' attention. Remember that everyone who looks through the classified section is a potential buyer. *They look at your ad because they choose to.*

When sitting down to write your small space ad, remember the goal: sell the product. When people look through the classifieds, they usually are looking for something that will satisfy some want or need. Your ad must in some way stand out from the rest of those inch wide, stackable sales pieces.

Now ask yourself this question: Would I buy my product? Hopefully, your answer is "yes." Now ask yourself, "why?" See for yourself the benefits your product or business has to offer. Be honest with yourself. Then, continue this honesty with your customers. Any other course of action will inevitably end in failure.

Again, your ad is stacked against dozens of others. What will make it stand out? A heading of some sort should do the job. The best bet would be to make it all capitalized, and in bold type if possible.

But what would the heading say? It must be something which is in the realms of describing the need or want of the reader. *The second they read that header, they should imagine themselves with that dream fulfilled.* For example, in areas where it is harder for people to own their own homes, a realtor who can provide this privilege may have a heading which reads:

OWN YOUR OWN HOME!

If I wanted to buy a house in an area where it was difficult, this heading would surely catch my attention. How about you? This method is often described as a

hook. Now the question is on how to "reel" them in.

All right, I'm a realtor, and I just bought an area of land upon which I am in the process of building houses. But to keep up progress in the construction, I want to get some people who will be willing to buy now and move in when we're ready. I am trying to get people to come to my office and allow me to show them some of the houses we already have completed. The point is that after reading the heading, I need to generate interest in what I have to offer.

OWN YOUR OWN HOME!
We have dozens of new homes
waiting to be bought.
One of them could be yours!
Call NOW! 555-5678
(name of company w/logo)

An ad, no matter how big or small, must motivate the reader to act. In the case of a small ad, the required purpose would be to either induce the reader to obtain further information about your product (i.e., to stimulate curiosity) or to go right ahead and buy it.

Further information can be gained in many different ways. If the company is a local business, the potential customer can call the business for further inquiry, or go to where it is located. If the business is out of town, information can be written for, or obtained via an 800 telephone number.

There are many other methods, especially in **display advertising,** where the ad is sold by the space, not by the word. Catchy illustrations or graphic designs in display ads can also get the reader's attention. Just be sure that the illustration has something to do with the product, otherwise it will lose its integrity. If an ad marketing a new pair of shoes catches my eye with a picture of a girl in a bathing suit, I'm not going to have much respect for the advertiser. Such methods are considered cheap.

Stimulating interest and desire rests with how much the reader thinks that the product will benefit them. A constant, positive, "you" emphasis must be maintained. Always write for the benefit of the reader. These benefits must be tangible. Stick only with the facts about your product, don't exaggerate, and don't promise too much. People are not stupid. If your ad promises something which is beyond believable, they're likely to laugh and turn to the next page. When you write your ad, be sure that your product will deliver what you promised.

To motivate the reader to act on buying the product or obtaining more information, the steps should be as effortless as possible. The easiest way for the reader to act is to call an 800 number. Although the phone companies offer these services at a surprisingly reasonable rate, this is something to be added only after business expands.

In small space advertising, coupons are perhaps the most valuable resource an advertiser can utilize. Whatever the sacrifice in price on your behalf, it will be well worth it, providing enough of the coupons get around.

The main question to be asking yourself when writing an ad is "HOW CAN MY PRODUCT OR SERVICE BENEFIT THE READER?" Ask others, as well. Get as many opinions as possible, not only on the benefits, but its possible drawbacks. Just remember, BE HONEST WITH YOURSELF, AND BE HONEST WITH YOUR READERS.

Judging Its Effectiveness

Many people who advertise in print utilize more than one publication. This presents a dilemma: which ad brought in the most business?

Therefore, you must find a way to test your ads. Here is another priceless benefit of using coupons. If your customers are responding by mail, there is a very simple way to test it. Designing or wording each ad in each publication with subtle differences. If there is a response coupon, then you can design that to each publication, and if they simply mail in a request, a process called **coding** should be used. This is when you write out your business address (or P.O. Box) differently, such as adding a letter after the street number, like 463-A Bellwood and 463-B Bellwood. Another technique is to slightly misspell the name of your street. Just look at your address and decide what you could modify to distinguish different ad responses.

The post office usually recognizes codes, so they shouldn't get lost. This way, you know which ads are bringing in the most business.

Chapter
5

Writing Copy

This chapter deals with the aspects of **copywriting**. The term **copy** as a noun, refers to the actual text contained within an ad, ranging from the headline to the paragraphs of small print describing the product that the ad is selling.

When performing this task, whether you're a professional copywriter or just trying to assemble a small ad for your small business, the words must be chosen with extreme care. It is not something to be performed indiscriminately, without thought.

Two aspects of words need to be considered here. The first is a word's **denotation**. By this, we are referring to the word's literal dictionary meaning, of which there may be several. The second thing to keep in mind is the word's **connotation**. This term refers not to the dictionary definition, *but how the public interprets it.*

Many words have different meanings in different geo-graphic locations, or some may be more popular (or just more positive in general) than others (For instance, the terms "pop" and "soda" both have roughly the same meanings. But in the southern states, "pop" is almost exclusive. Many Southerners tend to refrain from using "soda," thus making it easy to spot people from the north).

If you take a close examination of many print ads, especially those from magazines, you will notice a lot of common words, such as *free, guarantee,* and *new.* These are just a few examples. One of the most important things to remember is to not get too com-plicated. Say as much as possible in as few words as possible. Keep it simple. Key words such as those examples given, which usually carry seductive conno-tations, can be useful in creating an effective advertising piece.

Developing An Approach

There are two ways to promote a product. One method is called the **soft sell**. The soft sell is used mostly with luxury items, such as perfume, certain brands of clothing, and sports cars. You've probably seen these ads. They rely heavily on images of fantasy (the viewers', they hope), and give little information on any tangible benefits that the product has to offer.

The other form is the **hard sell**, which is used on most other products, such as food, toiletries, tools, and other types of cars and clothing. They appeal more to the audience's sense of logic, and present clear, straight-forward benefits of the product being promoted.

When similar products of different brands compete with each other, often there is the dilemma of making one product look superior to that of the competitor's. As a copywriter for your business, your goal may not necessarily be to find something unique or super about your product, for you may not find it. Chances are, it probably doesn't exist. There may be dozens of products on the market which could satisfy the customer as well as yours.

But the secret of making a product *appear* unique is to find a benefit which may be taken for granted, or go unnoticed. In some cases, this "benefit" may not even be real or practical, yet the sound of it is appealing (Just what does it mean to be a member of "the Pepsi Generation?"). Regardless, your next job is to make this angle exclusive to your own product.

Saying as much in as little as possible is one of the greatest challenges you may face as your own copywriter. Another is the variety of people you usually wind up writing to, even in the special interest publications. Not everyone may believe your ad, and may never be willing to get past the main heading.

Whatever your business may be, there is probably a good chance that you may hold some level of expertise in that field. If you run a sporting goods store, you probably have a good deal of knowledge of sporting goods and the interests the majority of your customers have. If you own a pet store, you hopefully know a lot about various kinds of pets and how to take care of them. This gives you an edge above the average copywriter who is used to writing ads for all sorts of clients (although some do have expertise in some fields from experience of writing for them).

Research

One of the major kinds of research you must conduct in order to create effective copy is, as reviewed in the first chapter, **market research**. This is an analysis of your product and who would want to buy it. You must ask yourself the following:

1) What does my product have to offer?
2) How can the customer benefit from use of it?
3) What would life be like without my product?
4) Will the customer be able (or willing) to pay the asking price?
5) Is there truly a difference between my product and the competitors'?
6) Who would be interested in my product?

From this information, you must find a **selling point**. For this task, you may need some outside assistance, such as family members or friends. Total strangers off the street would be even better. Since you probably know your product better than anyone else, you may not see it in the same perspective that someone else may. That is, *your product may have potential selling point that you may have never noticed*. But someone else can. Ask your customers who use the product already. Why do they keep coming back to it? Where would they go or what would they do if your product (or business) wasn't there for them? In asking these questions, you may hear a variety of answers. Make notes of them. You may never know some of the potential benefits your product may yield until you consult your regular consumers.

There are many clever tactics to giving your product appeal. One way of doing this is by tastefully citing a vice or disadvantage, and turning the tables on it. This is done commonly by comparing your product to another one which obviously may be better, but also more expensive, but then pointing out the inexpensiveness of your own.

If you are to write an effective ad, you must not only know a lot about your product, but who will use it. This can also be done through talking to the customers you have now (or to customers of competitors). You should have an idea of age, income, gender, major interests, occupation, and where they live. If, for instance, your user is a child, chances are the decision to buy is made by the parents. Your ad should target both these audiences.

Your Ad Theme

There are two distinctions which now must be made. This is between **customer benefits** and **selling points**. In advertising, which must have as much "you-emphasis" as possible, the themes should revolve around as many customer benefits as possible. Why? What's the difference? Although selling points can indeed be customer benefits, not all of them actually are. Looking for selling points occasionally is found through your point of view, not your customers'. This is why it is important to get some customers' points of view.

When someone looks at an ad, their only concern is how positively the product will affect them. Intrinsic worth is of little concern. Some questions they may ask may be whether it will make them happy (then again, what does?). How comfortable or what specific need does it satisfy, such as improving appearance or increasing popularity. Two other things which most people are seeking to increase: wealth and health.

This may sound like a bit much to expect of one product, and of course, not all these questions may be asked at one time. But, if you go through a magazine and look at the ads, you would be surprised at just how much other advertisers do promise with their products, and not just with words, but with images.

Nevertheless, whether you are promising a million dollars within 30 days, a more efficient appliance, or lower prices and better selection on all the goods in your store, your advertising approach must have a single focus. The focused benefit should be something which you are sure would interest a reader at a glance, getting him or her to keep their eyes glued to it. The heading should provide a sufficient hook. The subsequent text, and any instructions on how to obtain that product should not lose that central focus.

As stated before, advertising must have a very strong you-emphasis. We are living in the age of individualism. If a shampoo is more expensive, you're told to buy it anyway because you're "worth it." The most effective way of writing good "you" copy is to put yourself in your reader's place. Think back to when you were motivated by an ad for something. If it was for a business, they probably offered you the best selection and prices. If it was a product, it probably offered a direct benefit of some kind...a tangible benefit...one you could see yourself having moments after buying the product. Heed this attitude in writing your ad. Imagine yourself as your own customer. Put on their shoes and don't take 'em off till you're done writing.

Remember, you are targeting a specific audience with your ad. The appropriateness of it may differ, depending on what publications you are advertising in. An ad for one product in the daily newspaper (such as *The Pittsburgh Press*) may differ from that of the same product in the city's monthly magazine (such as *Pittsburgh Magazine*). A more specialized kind of people usually read the magazine, whereas many different people read the newspaper.

Another method is getting the reader involved in the ad. This can be done by asking the reader a question, or telling them to do something, in the headline. Suppose you owned a shoe store, and was planning a special sale—buy one pair of shoes at a regular price, get another for only $1 more. You could place a two part ad in the paper, the first part which read, "Name the only place in town where you can get a $30 pair of shoes for only $1." When they turn the page, you can lead them off with the name of your store, as well as more details on the special.

Guidelines to Follow

The following principles should aid you in creating a good sales piece. Of course, these principles are not absolute. Copywriting is much like art, and thus absolute rules inhibit its potential for effectiveness.

The first is choose your words with extreme care. As stated before, some words may be interpreted differently in different geographic locations. Don't choose words which you know will mislead your reader, because that is almost as bad as directly lying to them. It also gets consumers defensive, and justly so. But do indeed, within reason, pick the best words which will sell. After all, that is your goal. Pick words with positive connotations.

Next, be active in your voice. Don't use past tense unless you absolutely have to. "We're having a sale!" is better than "We've decided to have a sale!" It also uses fewer words.

Another thing to keep in mind is to write clearly. When first drafting it out, decide what you want to say, and say it. Don't worry about it being in the proper words at first. Lay your raw message down on paper first, then tinker with the choices. But don't stray from your initial message, and make sure that it remains the same throughout your rewriting.

Another thing to keep in mind is to remain concise. Say as much in as little as possible. But this rule can be broken in some instances. In direct marketing, the consumer can only get his or her information from the ad, and will want to know as much as possible before sending off a check. When the copy does become longer, pack it with relevant information. Allow the points to stride easily from one paragraph to the other.

Avoid the use of cliches as much as possible. Phrases which have been used to death, such as "new and improved," "while supplies last," "we guarantee it," and concept promises like "dreams coming true," and "for people like you," are heard over and over. Therefore, they may not hold an associative memory with your product in the reader's mind. Put simply, *your product won't stand out.* Of course, these phrases may be your only choice of words, if they fit your idea. By all means use what you must, but not to the point that they already have been used.

When taking a feature or a consumer benefit which may be taken for granted, be careful not to take the obvious and blow it up. If you sell refrigerators, you don't try to convince the customer that he needs your refrigerator to keep food cold. The customer knows that— that's why he wants one. Any refrigerator can satisfy that need. Explain what makes your refrigerator better than that of the competitors'. Price? Fringe benefits? Appearance? Size?

Your wording should be consistent with the language of the audience. By this we mean possible slang, light jargon associated with any special interest. Talk like two people interested in the same topic would talk to each other. This language should target your audience from the very beginning and hold them till the very end.

This may sound rather paradoxical, but as you write to a group, you should also try to keep the individual in mind. Just remember about conversation between two people who have a common interest. Keep up the you-attitude. This second person point of view will make the reader feel that they are in the middle of the action. Write off the top of your head. You might be surprised at how effective it can turn out.

ADVERTISING TECHNIQUES

The Testimonial

One of the most common, and oldest, forms of advertising is the **testimonial**. This is the process by which an individual, presumably famous and highly credible, is paid a handsome sum to endorse a product, usually on television, and quite frequently in print as well.

Of course, not just any celebrity can endorse any product. Much thinking goes into who is asked to do the endorsements. Bill Cosby is highly successful with Jell-0 Pudding commercials (and countless others, due to his high popularity) because of his wit and charm with children. Both kids and parents like him, and since kids eat the pudding and the parents buy it the ads target both audiences. General Mills, the producer of Wheaties cereal, have had dozens of famous athletes (usually Olympians) on their cereal boxes and in their commercials, promoting fitness and good health through the consumption of their cereal.

Humor

One thing to remember about humorous advertising: it either works tremendously, or it fails drastically. If you think that you have a good idea for a humorous ad, such as a pun or clever, witty angle, get as much feedback as possible before committing any money to it. It is generally accepted that most of the humorous ads which are thought up are not as good in print as they may have been to the copywriter at his or her desk.

Making Sense of the Ad

Besides the clever gimmicks and tricks to make your advertisement appealing, it must also contain a valid point in the message. You must give a good reason as to why the reader should want to buy your product.

For example, an ad for the BMW 535i Sports Sedan prides itself on having the performance of a sports car, and the practicality (being four-door) of a family car. Readers interested in obtaining an automobile (particularly of this brand) which offers both these features will find the ad for the car intriguing.

A magazine ad for Crest Toothpaste has a heading which is to the point, simply stating that independent studies prove that the fluoride system in Crest is better. It then breaks down into specific studies, showing the results.

Both these ads get straight to the point. There are no gimmicks or puns. The headlines aren't even fancy. They lay it out like it is, with crystal clear images of the product.

If you're running a sale of some kind, it might make more sense to explain why—therefore making the point more believable than if you were to present it with no reason. A good example would be the advertisements which car dealers run in the late summer. This is about the time when they are clearing their lots to make way for next year's models. In order to do so, they slash prices drastically on last year's, and run big campaigns for them in the process.

The Price of Dishonesty

It is commonly believed among most advertisers that truth is the best approach in advertising. This does not only include the exclusion of blatant lies but also ads which purposely mislead the reader. An ad should have a headline which appeals to a specific benefit to the reader—but the benefit must be real. If you start a practice of printing lies or wild exaggerations, it may bring a flow of immediate patronage, who, when given time, will discover the true integrity of your advertising. You will then have built a reputation for dishonesty, and such a reputation is very difficult to shake.

Writing Your Headline

Of course, the best copy in the world will inevitably go to waste if the reader isn't drawn into reading your ad. There are two basic aspects which perform this function. One is design, and the other is the headline.

Your headline must be the first thing for the audience to read. It should be short and to the point. It can be a straight sentence, or a slogan, a pun, or a rhyme of some sort.

But one very important task of the headline: not only must it get their attention, but it must *motivate them to act*. This can be done in many ways. A headline can make them a promise, give a command, or illustrate a user benefit.

The line can also be straight-forward as well, with nothing fancy. Mercedes Benz advertised its cars as "Rated the safest car in America."

Whatever your headline or copy, remember that how well your product or business might sell depends largely upon the information and the clarity with which it is delivered. The consumer wants to know as much about the product as possible. Although it can be beneficial by using clever slogans and literary tricks to deliver a general appeal and sense of taste and style, don't allow yourself to indulge upon it. Remember, you are delivering information to sell a product. That is the overall purpose. I have seen ads which are done so cleverly and entertainingly to the point where they have overshadowed the product that they were selling. In other words, after the ad was finished, or after I had turned the page, quite often I would not remember what was being sold.

If you can write well, good. But remember: **Write to Sell.**

Chapter 6

Public Relations

During the author's first years of college, he took a summer job as a delivery boy for a small pizza shop in a suburb of Pittsburgh, Pennsylvania. Early that summer, there was a violent rainstorm which caused massive flooding. Millions of dollars worth of damage was done, and many families' homes were ruined. The shop was right in the vicinity, and in the following weeks, they made a practice of taking free pizzas (by the stack) down to the relief area, for the victims and the workers.

Why did they do this? They didn't get paid for them. There weren't any close friends or employees who were hit hard by the disaster.

The answer was simple: as a member of the community, it was their moral obligation (and privilege) *to utilize their resources to help those other members of the community in need. This is one of the most highly stressed beliefs of public relations practitioners.*

When one hears the term **public relations,** one tends to see the stereotypical image of corporate communications departments, men and women standing before swarming reporters trying to answer difficult questions in the midst of a corporate crisis.

That is only one side of public relations. Those situations do occasionally exist for those who practice in the corporate field. But today's companies are spending more and more money on public relations every year.

But it should not only be on the minds of corporate executives. Public relations (PR) is the concern of any business which operates within a community. *This means just about every business there is.*

Public Relations Defined

There are many definitions of public relations. An important goal on behalf of big business in PR is to make sure that the corporation *remains human.* It is awfully easy to stay in your office or place of business and be consumed by only by what will increase your profits, forgetting that there is a world outside, and human beings not only as customers, but employees as well.

So how would one define public relations? Of the many definitions, probably one of the best is the *process by which a company may, through the use of two-way communication, keep in touch with the feelings and*

*points of view of its employees and the general public,
and thereby acting on this information.*

For small business, public relations does not
usually involve extensively planned campaigns, and
you will probably never have to appear before a press
conference. For small business, public relations is an
attitude. It's an attitude which determines how much
a part of the community the small business wants to
make itself. It can succeed by making minor contri-
butions. A good example would be to help sponsor local
charitable events. Another would be to allow your
business to be utilized as a location where many people
gather. If you own a restaurant, you could post a
community bulletin board, so that the local customers
can see other (usually non-profit) events happening in
the area. There are many ways in which business can
benefit their community without having to go to a great
expense in doing so.

Opinions and Feedback

One of the most common duties of the public
relations profession is obtaining the general opinions of
the consumers and employees. In the larger sense,
massive polls and surveys are taken, but you as a small
business may want to consider something similar.

Here's an example: if you owned a small grocery
store in a neighborhood, and you were considering
expanding your service to delivering groceries to those
in the immediate area (within a radius of two or three
miles), who phoned in the request. For this service, you
would charge a nominal sum of a few dollars. But before
going to the expense of hiring on extra help to do so, you
need some questions answered: Would the public like

it? Would they take advantage of it? How do you find these answers?

Simple. Conduct a survey.

How? You could easily print up brief question-naires presenting your idea, and asking them whether or not they would use it. It wouldn't have to be more than three or four questions. You could ask your customers at the checkout to quickly fill them out before they leave. It probably wouldn't take them more than 30 seconds.

One thing to remember, though. When making out a questionnaire, write the questions as objectively as possible. By this we mean, don't write the question so it anticipates the respondent's answer.

There is an also another invaluable public relations tool to be used here. Suppose you were to offer the same service, but FREE to those senior citizens who cannot travel easily?

You may find yourself gaining customers you've never had! And you would be providing a great service to the community. Since you would be operating within an immediate area, you could photocopy a few hundred fliers and distribute them around the neighborhoods, and in grocery bags of customers who do come to your store. This would start off a good local campaign which would further be spread by word of mouth.

"Free" Advertising

What was once referred to as "free" advertising, is today called **publicity.** Publicity can be obtained by issuing a simple document called a **news release**, which contains possibly newsworthy information in ready-to-publish form. Often, depending on how they are written, they are printed in the newspapers exactly as they are received, or bits and pieces are taken out of collected news releases and combined into a single column of miscellaneous information.

Whether or not they are printed at all depends on the judgement of the editor on how interested the public may be.

Suppose you were expanding the size of your business, or were offering some new novelty product or service. Some years ago, a Pittsburgh video retailer and renter teamed up with a neighboring pizza shop (not the same one as before) and offered a "pizza and movie" deal: both items to be delivered at your door by the same driver. Both managers got together and sent news releases to the local papers and TV stations. Not only did this result in a major feature article in a section of the following Sunday's Pittsburgh Press, but one of the local stations did a TV news story on them the very day they sent out the releases!

The Format of the News Release

Whether you format your release correctly literally determines whether or not the editor throws it in the trash or prints it in the paper. Newspapers (and TV stations) receive hundreds to thousands of news releases each week, of which only a few will be printed. But a common way of filtering out to the good ones is by immediately throwing away those which are typed incorrectly or have obvious errors. The following rules set forth the correct format in which news releases

THE PALMER-DONAVIN MFG. COMPANY

GENERAL OFFICES

FAX (614) 486-5073   1200 Steelwood Road   (800) 589-4412

Columbus, Ohio 43212-1372

(614) 486-9657

Service is our most important product

FOR IMMEDIATE RELEASE

May 1, 1990

Contact:

Bob Woodward, Chairman of the Board

Alan Vogt, President, Heating and Air Conditioning Division

Ron Calhoun, President, Building Materials Division

Thursday, May 3, 1990, marked The Palmer-Donavin Mfg Co.'s Open House Celebration, introducing their new facility at 1200 Steelwood Rd. in Columbus, Ohio, which consolidates three formerly separate operating divisions: Building Materials, Heating & Air Conditioning, and Cabinets.

Those in attendance of the Open House saw first hand the new facility, and learned how it will allow the people of Palmer-Donavin to better serve their customers. Over 50 exhibitors were on hand showing the latest products in their lines for the 1990's.

The new location, a 148,000 square foot office and warehouse on approximately nine acres of land, utilizes the very latest in technology to manage receiving, storing, and shipping of materials quickly and efficiently.

Also being celebrated was Palmer-Donavin's Anniversary of 83 years of service. In that time, Palmer-Donavin has gone from supplying macaroni and pots & pans to becoming a primary source of building materials, heating and air conditioning supplies, and cabinets, for businesses throughout Ohio.

In addition to the Columbus facility, Palmer-Donavin has branches in Lima and Cincinnati, and employs a team of 150 men and women.

#####

BUILDING MATERIALS	CABINET DIVISION	LIMA BRANCH	HEATING & COOLING	CINCINNATI BRANCH
1200 Steelwood Rd.	1200 Steelwood Rd.	1245 Neubrecht Rd.	1200 Steelwood Rd.	2996 Exon Avenue
Columbus, OH 43212	Columbus, OH 43212	Lima, OH 4580*	Columbus, OH 43212	Cincinnati, OH 45241
(614) 486-1223	(614) 486-7447	(419) 225-2045	(614) 486-0975	(513) 583-2000
(800) 589-3223	(800) 589-7447	(800) 472 4949 OH	(800) 686 0975	(800) 686-3212
FAX (614) 486-8101	FAX (614) 486-8101	(800) 537-5370 IN	FAX (614) 486-5037	FAX (513) 563-1659
		FAX (419) 229-1258		

Figure 6-1. *An example of a news release (courtesy of The Palmer-Donavin Manufacturing Company).*

should be submitted:

1) Standard 8–1/2" by 11" paper should be used. Nothing expensive, just use standard copy paper, or your business stationary. It should be double-spaced, on one side only. Margins should be at about an inch to an inch and a half all around. It should definitely not be more than two pages, and it's best to try to keep it on one. The goal of newspaper writing is to say as much as you can in as few words as possible. Remember that when writing.

2) Your name, business, address and phone number should be at the top of the release. You should include both work and home phone numbers of the writer in case the editor has any questions. It's even better to list two individuals, with phone numbers, who are familiar with the ad in case one cannot be reached.

3) Include a release date, which indicates that the story is either for "immediate" release or to be held until the date posted.

4) In journalism, there are what are called **slug lines**. These are marks at the bottom of the page to indicate either the end of the release (which is simply "####" at the end) or to continue to the next page (the word "more" at the bottom). Headlines can be written in, also, but they will probably be used for the editors' reference. Chances are the copy editors will write the printed headline themselves, accounting the space given.

5) One of the most important things to remember are newspaper deadlines. Everything in news journalism revolves around the deadlines. If the deadline is 4:00

and a story is handed in at 4:01, it will have to wait until the next edition, and by then your release may well be "old news."

While many PR firms and departments make a practice of mailing releases to papers and stations, it is usually better to personally deliver it to the editor or producer. If you don't feel you have the time to do this yourself, determine if there are local messenger services which can deliver your release for you. Depending on the size of your community, these services may be able to make deliveries within an hour or two after receipt.

If you begin dealing with a certain department of a newspaper or TV station, it will help to get to know the individuals who work there. And always keep up with who is in what position. If Bob Smith recently replaced Jane Rogers as the editor, he is not going to be impressed by a release still addressed to Jane. If you are not sure of the current editor's name, simply call newspaper or TV station and ask the receptionist. After delivering the release, you might want to follow up with a phone call at least to make sure that they read your release.

Finally, if you've given it your best shot, and the press refuses to run your story, don't worry about it. Don't be offended. And don't keep bugging them. This will just make you a nuisance, and if you send in another release on something different months later, they may toss it simply because you got on their nerves the first time. Many times editors and producers don't include certain released items simply because of other occurrences which need priority coverage. In simpler terms, your release has the best chances on a slow news day.

On Writing A News Release

In journalism, there is the simple method of writing which tends to dominate the stories found in newspapers. This is called the **inverted pyramid.** The purpose of this is, as stated before, to say as much as you can in as few words as possible.

Journalists want to answer as much of the following in the first paragraph of a story: Who, what, where, when, how, and why. This way, when placing the story in the paper, the editors can simply chop off from the bottom up if they have to, and still won't lose the essence of the story. So when writing a release, remember:

1) List all important facts, answering the questions above.

2) Try to squeeze that information in the first two paragraphs.

3) Keep the paragraphs short and concise (not more than 6 or 7 lines). Avoid flowery language.

4) A good reference, if you find yourself writing more releases, is the *Associated Press Stylebook and Libel Manual.* It is a good reference book for determining how certain names, places and subjects are depicted in the press (For instance, how should I depict *General Electric?* Can I just say "GE", or must I write it out?). A copy of this useful book may be obtained in many bookstores, especially those on college campuses, or by sending a check for $8.75 to Stylebook—AP Newsfeatures, 50 Rockefeller Plaza, New York, NY

10020. Make checks payable to "AP Stylebook."

Public relations is not just for big business. It's for *all* business. The press is very receptive to those who have some interesting stories and opportunities for the public to hear about. And the best part about it is, *it's FREE.*

Chapter 7

Basic Black & White Design and Production

Equally important as the words that go into an ad are the images it displays. There are many aspects of advertising design which largely decide whether or not an individual will stop to look at the ad. When beginning your own ad campaign, without the use of an agency, there are certain basics you may want to know about **design** (the craft of layout and art) and **production** (the craft of preparing the camera ready ad).

This chapter will introduce you to basic accepted concepts of design and production of black and white, camera ready ads which would be used for newspaper and magazine classified advertising. While most newspapers provide a layout service at no extra charge, the quality of the results often reflects its price. Full color ads, which contain photos and professional designs, are prepared similarly, yet require a bit more explaining. It may also be harder to understand until you have gotten accustomed to elementary black and white production.

There are very few businesses which do not have a **logo** of some sort. This is the name of the business used in a special type of design which is to be seen in all forms of advertising, business cards, and stationary. As far as the general public is concerned, when they see the **logo**, *they see the company.* It is the one thing which must remain consistent at all times in order to work.

Your Goal As A Business

Your goal as a business is, of course, to make money. You do this by increasing clientele. This in turn must be done by getting their attention.

How do you do that? First, find out what gets *your* attention. Go to the nearest newspaper, magazine, or Yellow Pages. Spend time paging through them, casually. Don't look for anything to catch your eye...let it do that naturally. If you find yourself automatically scrutinizing everything you see, try *flipping* through the pages. Have you ever done that and then found yourself going back to find an image which caught your eye for a quarter of a second? What was it about that image which acquired your attention with such limited exposure?

Each time you come across an ad or a logo which you think is successful, cut it out. Do this as often as possible. Ask your friends and family to help, too. Anyone who has eyes is qualified. It requires no formal training. Design is geared to attract the attention of *everyone*, not just art critics. You are literally conducting an experiment each time you flip through those pages. And the more often an experiment is conducted, the more accurate are the results it yields.

After you have enough clippings, lay them out and examine them. Why did you choose these? Was it the logos themselves or the layout of the ads? These are things which you will have to consider when designing your own logos and ads.

Logos As Messages

Just imagine what design has done for business and industry as a whole. In the most successful cases, it is hard to hear the business's name without an image coming to mind. I'll give three examples: McDonald's, AT&T and Twentieth Century Fox. For these names, and hundreds of others, the logos go hand in hand with the names. When you hear the name, you see the logo, and vice versa.

Logos not only imply a name, they also convey a message. The Mercedes Benz star is also considered a symbol for fine craftsmanship and engineering in automobiles. With these implications already generally accepted, few or no words are needed when the logo is displayed in an ad.

Whatever the logo you may choose, you must feel comfortable with it. It will represent your business, and should eventually become symbolic of it.

Basic Tools of Design

After you have gone through enough of the ads in the newspaper or magazine, you may start to get an idea of how you may want your ad to look. Don't put off getting these ideas down on paper. The following design tools are a few essentials you will need in order to draft and finish your own advertisements. They are the following:

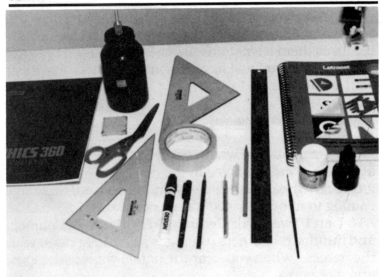

Figure 7-1. Some of the items you may need to for conventional paste-up.

1) *A sketch pad.* Bienfang brand Graphics 360 series is perhaps your best choice. Since you will be using an art marker to sketch, and even some final work, this paper allows the finest edges and the best absorbency. They come in many sizes, and a good choice for you would be 9 by 12 inches, or perhaps a bit larger.

2) *A ruler, triangles and compass.* An 18 inch ruler, preferably made of steel, and clear plastic triangles, one 45/45/90 degrees and the other 30/60/90 degrees. A simple drawing compass (or a circular template) may come in handy if you need to draw any circles.

3) *Pencils, plastic eraser and a black marker.* For doing sketches, art pencils may be better than conventional No.2's. They are rated by softness; H (hard) pencils ranging from H to H8 (H8 being the hardest), and B (soft) pencils going up to B6 (which is softest, and the darkest). The best choice for you may be an HB (right in between) and a 2H (just a bit harder). A plastic eraser, not a rubber one, does the cleanest job for production work. A black art marker, both thick– and thin–lined, may also be beneficial in doing compositions.

4) *Non-photo blue pencils.* A few of these pencils are good to have. They are best when used lightly on mechanical images (to draw in outlines and such) and won't show on film.

5) *A Letraset Catalogue.* There are many manufacturers of **presstype,** which are letters that you rub down on **illustration board** (see below), in the position that you want them, and a common brand is Letraset. Every year, they print a large, spiral catalogue of graphic arts supplies, many of which are hundreds of different typefaces. When photocopied up or down to the sizes you want, these can be a great resource in doing sketches for final advertisements.

6) *Black ink pen and white-out.* There are many types of technical pens, all varying greatly in price. You should try for an inexpensive, fine line, dark India ink pen. The local art and drafting supply stores will have plenty to choose from. You may also wish to get white retouch paint and a "0000" (very fine) brush.

7) *Scissors, tape, rubber cement (or hot-waxer) and pickup.* Since the majority of the work will be

simple paste-up, these supplies will be needed. Rubber cement (and a jar to keep it in), or hot wax are the best for this kind of work, and a "pickup", made of the same material, will easily pick up excess cement on the areas of the board to remain clean.

8) *Illustration board.* There are many kinds of illustration board. **Cold press** is very rough and absorbent. The type you want, **hot press**, is smooth, and very white. There are many types of this, as well. Your local dealer should be able to recommend the type most suitable for your purpose, depending on the brand carried.

9) *Matte knife and cutting board.* Since illustration board is usually purchased in sheets of 15 by 20 inches or larger, you'll need to cut out a piece the specific size that you want. The board may be a simple piece of chip board, about the size of a game board, found in lumber stores.

All of these items can be found in art supply and drafting stores. If you have any questions on picking one of two similar items, the dealers there should be able to help you out.

Designing Your Own Logo

As mentioned before, your business logo is one of the most important aspects of your overall advertising campaign. Chances are, if your business is already off the ground, you may have one. If this is the case, this section will inform you on how to change it if you want to, or to simply have your logo on hand for future print advertisements.

Since the majority of small space ads are black and white, your logo should reproduce efficiently in this medium. But it can still be rather decorative if you wish. It can be a cartoon character, or a symbol of some sort. Do rough sketch ideas in pencil. Then take the ones you like and redo them in marker. Get outside input. Be flexible. Don't be hesitant to change something you may have fallen in love with in the first drafting. But before you commit to a final sketch, be sure to get plenty of opinions. *Don't just show others your favorite one, and ask, "How do you like this?" Show it to them with plenty of other perspective logos and ask, "Which one do you like?" Don't point out your favorite; let them choose theirs.*

A logo does not necessarily have to be a symbol. It can simply be the business name in a specific type, either taken right from a type book, or from a custom designed typeface. Some of the nicest ones are that of a combination, with the symbol placed with the name in a designerly fashion. You can experiment with different kinds of typefaces. Look through your type book and choose three or four potential type styles that you would be interested in seeing your business name in. Take them to a Xerox machine, and enlarge them around 150 to 200 percent. Take a sheet of graphics paper and, on a clean table under a good light, trace your name in those letters. If you find a style you like, you can design your logo so it will match up with it.

Once you have reached a design with which you are pleased, you are now ready to prepare the camera ready piece. By this time, you should have a finely tuned sketch of your design on graphics paper. If you don't, you will have to complete one, but without the type.

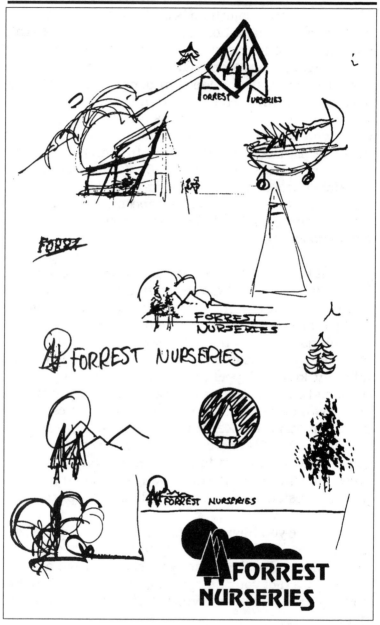

Figure 7-2. Examples of logo sketches, with the final along the bottom.

Figure 7-3. Markers are the best medium when doing rough layouts, be it for full ads or just logos.

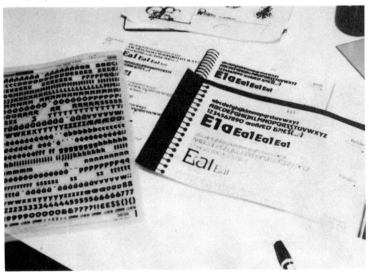

Figure 7-4. Type may be sketched from a Letraset Catalogue. Then the font may be purchased on sheets, which you press down onto the board (Letraset is just one brand of presstype...there are many others as well.)

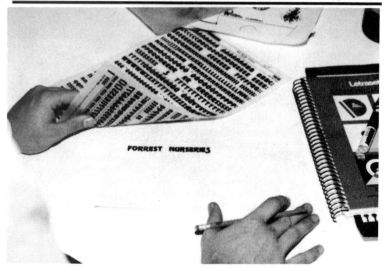

Figure 7-5. You can press out any name or word that you want, in virtually any font you wish.

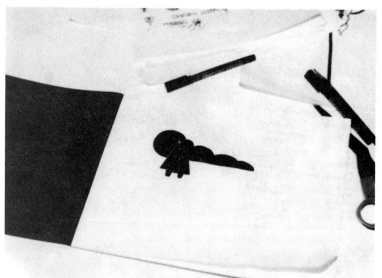

Figure 7-6. Your graphic image finely tuned, after doing many sketches.

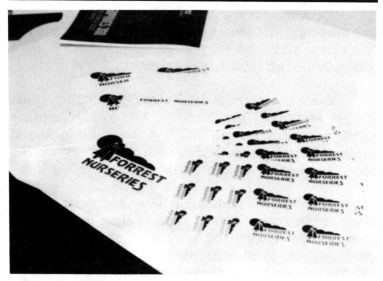

Figure 7-7. From there you combine graphic images and type to produce your own logo sheets, with the aide of a good copier. However, for finer reproductions, PMT's are recommended.

On a sheet of graphics paper, make a large pencil line drawing. The size should be at least three inches. The image must be as perfect as possible. Use a compass and straight-edges where applicable.

Once the image is done with pencil, take the art marker, and color it in solid black. Be very careful of the edges, as well. You can still use straight edges, and circles can be done neatly if you fill in slowly around the edge, one tiny stroke at a time.

Any minor mistakes can be whited out using the white acrylic paint. It should be as close to perfect as possible. Don't worry too much, though, because this image is going to be reduced, and that will help make any flaws less noticeable.

Assuming you have chosen a typeface to letter your company name, purchase a sheet of presstype for that font and size which corresponds correctly to your logo. On a separate sheet of paper, press out your name, but be sure to space each word apart enough so that they can be cut out and arranged the way you want with the logo.

After the name is pressed out, find a really good copier. This is very important. Copiers vary greatly in the quality of their reproductions, and it is imperative that you get a good one. Professional copy shops have plenty of copiers to use, and most of them only charge about a nickel a copy. Seek one out that suits you, and keep on using it.

Next, copy the pressed out name. You will cut out the copy, *not the original.* Now place the words on the sheet with the logo. Once you have them arranged, brush rubber cement on both the paper with the logo, and the other sides of the words (it may be easier to brush the words before you cut them out). It will take the cement a few seconds to dry. Once it has, carefully place the words down. If you make a mistake, simply peel it up and re-cement a little bit. Use the pickup to take off excess cement.

Now you will need to make up several *logo sheets*. While printers tend to charge a significant amount for this service, you can do it yourself with a good copier at very little cost. You may want at least two sizes of the logo to make up your sheet. This is done by making multiple reductions on the copier. If you look at the photo in Figure 7-7, six copies of one reduction and nine of the other, smaller reduction were made, then cut out, cemented down on a clean sheet, and recopied several times (if the copier tends to show cut paper lines, white-out can take care of that—but if you utilize the services of copy shops, which would be your best bet, they will probably have a very sophisticated machine that will copy paste-ups without those lines). In a just a few minutes, bang! Instant logo sheets.

The logos on these sheets are what you will cut out to place in your advertisements. These methods may sound rather unconventional, and unprofessional by some peoples' standards, but for your purpose, they provide the fastest, most economical way of getting the job done.

Putting Together Your Ad

The procedure of laying out an ad is not much different than was that of laying out your logo sheet.

The principles are the same.

Of course, there are many things to consider when designing your own ad. What's the size? Is it just black and white? (For our example we will assume it is.) Will you offer coupons? How much copy will there be? What can you do to make your ad appealing, even if it is black and white?

You may find yourself drawing a blank. That's what those other ads are for. Look at them again. What do you like about them? Is it the type? An illustration? Basic layout?

What makes up a design? What makes it unique, and effective?

1) *Line.* This can be made up of solid black borders, the type, and any designed shapes. Black and white ads are commonly referred to as **"line art."**

2) *Tone.* Even in black and white advertising, you can still have grays. Presstone (made up of dots) can be obtained, at any shade, at any art and drafting store.

3) *Direction.* This is something to be discussed in more detail later. But remember this: the more defined the direction, the more dynamic, and consequently, the more effective, your ad may be.

4) *Shape.* This can be judged by looking at the ad from afar, and blurring your vision of it. What kinds of shapes do you make out of the lines? The logos? The blocks of type?

Now let's assume that you want to design a small black and white ad to be placed in the classifieds of a magazine or newspaper. When beginning your own ad campaign, it is best to start small and increase the ambitiousness of your advertisements as your profits increase. However, if you want to and have the capital to start out printing larger, even perhaps full page, ads, the same technical principles still apply.

Let's assume that you want to print an ad in a rectangle that is 4 inches by 6 inches (in classified advertising that is not simply stacked type, which is usually sold by the letter, ad space is sold by the inch or half inch). You have your pitch and your copy written (see Chapter Five). Your logo is designed and you have the appropriate size to cut out from your logo sheet.

It is at this point where you may be quite puzzled. You look at the ads in the newspapers and magazines and see how the copy is typeset in a font which is relatively consistent with that of the logo or the rest of the ad. Your copy may be final in the way you want it, but how do you typeset it yourself? How do you get your words from a typewritten sheet of paper to that of a final, professional looking copy block?

The Priceless Role of Computers

If you happen to own a computer, you are blessed.

If you don't, many copy stores and printers have computers for patron use, or they can typeset the text themselves, if you wish it. Almost all typesetting today is done through the use of computers. Word processing and graphics programs have many typefaces to choose from, and can be printed onto any kind of paper by the use of laser printers.

There are now many computer systems available to perform these functions. Not only will they typeset copy, but with the use of such software (available for both IBM and Apple Macintosh computer systems) as *Aldus PageMaker, Aldus Freehand, Quark Xpress,* and Letraset's *Ready, Set, Go!,* **you can produce camera-ready advertisements without even touching a pair of scissors!**

This is the world of **desktop publishing.** A complete system can run you anywhere from five to ten thousand dollars, but today, more and more companies, big and small, are making this highly innovative, and worthwhile investment.

As stated above, entire ads quite often are done on computer via desktop publishing programs, totally eliminating the need for paste-up. These programs possess both word processing (typing in different fonts) and graphics (drawing ability) capabilities. As a matter of fact, if you have a clean copy of your logo on paper, you can have it *scanned,* or "read" into the computer, which will then reproduce it perfectly, and at any size and proportion you wish! **Scanning** simply converts the image into digital language that the computer will understand in order to produce it.

If you already own a computer, even if you don't have a laser printer, it would still be in your best interest to pay a visit to your local software dealer and explore the options available to you, according to your needs. An investment of not more than a few hundred dollars addition to your present computer may be well worth it.

Once your ad is designed and stored on a disk, you can take it to a shop which feature laser printers that can print your ad for a nominal charge, probably not much more than a photocopy.

However, when using conventional paste-up, have your copy (and heading, as well) typeset and printed on plain white sheets, you may want to get several copies of it made, either through the printer or just by taking it to a photocopy machine and running them off there. If you do not yet know the exact size of the final ad or the arrangement of the copy in it (and chances are you won't), then you may want to make several photocopy enlargements and reductions of your text, to give you flexibility in experimenting with different designs and layouts.

Another method of having type laid out for your ad is through an electric daisy wheel typewriter. Different fonts can be purchased, and many of them are useful for ads. Letter Gothic is a particularly suitable font, when just starting out.

What About Illustrations?

Are you selling a particular product? Is it and others like it on sale? Chances are you are not an illustrator, but you do have many options at your disposal. Open your Letraset catalogue or visit your local art and drafting store. They will have many **clip art** books and presstype graphics of images and pictures of all sorts, all of which are camera ready and available for you to print as often as you wish. One excellent resource for clip art are the *Graphic Source* clip art produced by the Graphic Products Corporation. They can be found in many bookstores and art stores, of various subjects.

Note: *Do NOT present a generic image of a product to be that of a specific brand. For example, you can print generic pictures of electronic equipment, such as VCR's. But these images CANNOT be used to advertise a SPECIFIC brand and model, such as one made by Sony or General Electric. They can be used however, to advertise your whole inventory in general.*

If you are a dealer of brand name products, you can probably obtain camera ready illustrations and pictures from the manufacturer. Most often, if selling a specific brand, the manufacturer will share the costs of the advertising (commonly referred to as **cooperative advertising**).

What About Photographs?

A black and white photograph can be inserted into a line art advertisement with relative ease. Photographs, like paintings, are **continuous–tone** art, and must therefore be converted over to line art by a printer, through a photomechanical process. Since line art is pure black and white, with no grays, a half-tone screen must be used to create the *illusion* of continuous tone, by the use of tiny dots, exactly the same way that the "presstone" gives the illusion of grey. (This is how all printing is done, even color. Color printing, although it creates a full color effect, only utilizes 3 to 4 colors: red, blue, yellow, and occasionally black. It is the mixture of these colors in varying degrees at the "dot" level which allows the representation of full color to appear.)

One thing to remember: the kind of screen used depends on the type of paper on which the final image

Figure 7-8. Samples of thumbnails.

will be printed. Halftone screens come in varying degrees, from 65 dots per inch all the way up to 300 dots per inch. Of course, the fewer dots per inch, the easier they are to see with the naked eye. If your ad is for a newspaper or anything on newsprint paper, you will want to use 65 to 85 dots per inch. Magazines, which use a slicker, glossier paper, would use around 150. A good printer will be able to advise you on the proper screen to use for what you have to shoot and where it will be printed.

As you move on, you will first learn how to do a simple mechanical with just line art, then how to integrate a black and white photograph into it.

DESIGNING YOUR LAYOUT

Now remember, the size of your ad was to be a 4 by 6 inch rectangle. From this point, you will go from a rough idea in your head to the final, camera ready piece, via three stages: thumbnail, composition, and final.

The Thumbnail Stage

Now open your graphics pad. Consider the elements to be found in your ad: headings, copy blocks, illustrations, and logos. You may have an idea of what you want your ad to look like already, but before beginning your mechanical, you should get that idea and at least a few more roughed out on paper.

Reach for your black marker. Sit down on the couch, or your bed, anywhere you can relax with your graphics pad in your lap. Very quickly, sketch out rectangles (any size) roughly proportional to what your ad will be. Don't be concerned about mistakes; at this stage, you can't make any.

Inside those rectangles, visualize the layout which your design will have. Believe it, there are many more designs than the conventional horizontal stacking of type. Look through some of the more dynamic ads which you may have chosen. By this term we mean ads which seem to move in one direction, or when all the type, copy, and graphic images (logos, illustrations, and photographs) appear to meld together into one whole shape.

Ask yourself how your ad may be just as dynamic. Don't hesitate to imitate (only to a certain degree, of course) an ad which appeals to you, for it is almost certain that ad was also inspired by something else similar. Art and design is the same as literature in this respect: *nothing is completely original.*

Keep on doing rough sketches of how your ad may look. These sketches are referred to as **thumbnails**. Doing these exercises allows you to organize all your elements as shapes interacting with each other, instead of separate elements competing for the viewer's attention. We stress the use of the term "shape". Everything has shape, and it is through this understanding which unique and attractive designs can flow from your imagination with relative ease.

The Composition Stage

Once you have found a sketch which you feel will work well in your ad, you are ready to move on to the composition stage. A **composition**, or "comp," is simply a more refined sketch, usually done the same size of the final mechanical.

Take your triangles, ruler and a pencil. Draw a rectangle 4 by 6 inches. It is here you have the option of using either a black marker, or just pencil. If there is no halftone involved, you may probably use a marker, but if there will be a halftone, then you might prefer just to use pencils (unless you wish to invest some money in grey markers, which range from 10 to 90 percent in value—but they aren't essential to your goals). Pencils can be useful in that you can get most *values* (meaning lightness or darkness) out of them.

Chances are the largest type will be your heading. This may already have been typeset along with your copy, if you have already decided on the font to be used. If not, you may choose a typeface from your type book and sketch it the same way you did with your business name (when doing your logo), although not in the same crispness—this is, after all, just a sketch.

When you know where you want the other graphic images to go, you may simply sketch them roughly onto the pad. They may not look like much up close, but from a relative distance, it gives a good representation of what the final ad will look like. Copy can simply be represented by straight lines, of the same approximate size, called "copylines."

Show your comp to others, and get plenty of input. If you have reached a layout which you think will prove effective, then you're ready to begin your mechanical.

The Final Stage

Now you have your design finished, and your layout completely organized. Next your job is to translate this design into a photo-ready mechanical to be given to the publication in which you will advertise.

Note: *Before handling the illustration board and any paper images to be photographed, make sure that your hands and work area are CLEAN. White board will amplify the slightest fingerprints.*

The first step in this process is to prepare your **mechanical board.** You will have to use the matte knife, metal ruler, and cutting board. The triangle can be used to insure that the cutting lines are square. After you have drawn out your piece to cut from one corner, lay the ruler on the board inside the piece to be cut out. When you cut with the knife, go gently, several strokes at a time. Don't press down too hard. That's how you get cuts.

Now take your non-photo blue pencil and a triangle. The 4 by 6 inch square of reference should be square to the edge of the board; that is, all of the lines should be exactly parallel to the edges of the board. This can be achieved by first drawing the horizontal lines (the top and the bottom) on the board. Center them by drawing each one, each 1–1/2 inches from either end. Don't worry about the lengths of the lines, just draw them from one edge of the board to the other.

Next, do the exact same thing with the vertical lines, each 1–1/2 inches from either end. You now have your rectangular **frame of reference** (the area to be photographed), the inside of which should be given the

Figure 7-9. *Copy can be typeset by computer, or even on a daisy-wheel typewriter.*

greatest discretion when being handled. It must remain as spotless as possible.

Your next task is to take an ink pen, which produces as crisp lines as possible, and carefully, with a ruler, draw **cropmarks** along the lines at each corner outside the frame of reference (see Figure 7-13). You should have the inside edge of each cropmark end about one forth to one half inch from the edge of the frame of reference. The length of the cropmark should be about one inch long.

You should now have your elements which will go inside the frame of reference (logos, heading, blocks of type, illustrations, photos) already printed on separate sheets of paper. All you have to do now is cut them

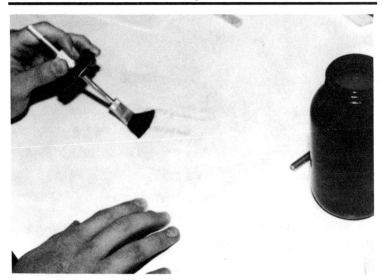

Figure 7-10. *Use rubber cement or hot wax to adhere strips of paper to the illustration board.*

out and paste them down on the board in the arrangement you want them (except for the photo—more on that later).

Rubber cement or hot wax are the best substances to use when producing mechanicals. Rubber cement is brushed on both surfaces, which of course, must remain dry and clean. The best way to avoid messiness is to rubber cement to opposite sides of the images to be cut out before your cut them out. Remember, if you lay the letters down and they aren't right, you can gently peel them up and set them down again. You'll get the hang of it.

Now when you have a photograph, there are two ways of preparing it for the mechanical. The first is to have a line copy transferred version of the photo (as

Figure 7-11. Clip art books can be a great source of copyright free illustrations.

explained earlier) printed on a paper called "velox" cut to the exact size to appear on the mechanical. If this is the case, it can go directly on the mechanical, since it is line art just as the other elements.

If you don't have a line version of the photo, you can make a heavy black or red **holding line** around the exact area in which the photograph will lie.

With the holding lines on the first mechanical, the actual photo will go on another. It is set up the exact same way, with frame of reference lines and crop marks, all in the exact same spaces. Only with this one, the only other image to go on the board is the photo itself, with cropmarks at each corner the same way you have it on the outside.

Figure 7-12. You can preserve your book by using and cutting photocopies from the original pages.

Now after these few simple steps have been completed, you may want to inspect it for any obscure marks or lines along the edges of cut paper, which may accidentally show up in the final printing itself. White retouch paint and a small, "0000" size brush, is all you need to make these corrections.

Now take your finished work to your printer. Ask him to make a **photostat** (i.e., a reproduction of it on photographic paper). You will receive a stat in return which will be of the exact size that will appear in the publication. This photostat, or a good photocopy of it, will be what you give to the publication for printing.

Of course, you do have other options. It is not absolutely necessary to have a photostat made—in

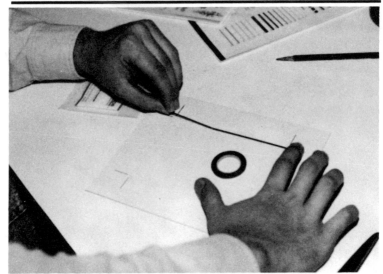

Figure 7-13. *Graphic line tape can be used for creating boxes and rectangles, or even just graphic accents.*

some cases, a photocopy may do just as well. But generally stats are better. They give much crisper results. You can also give the publication the actual mechanical you finish yourself, but with the work you put into it, I think that it is in your best interest to keep that on hand, and allow only stats and copies to change hands.

How The Mechanical Works

In preparing graphic work to be printed, you have only two colors: black and white. When mechanicals are shot, a photographic negative is produced on which, as you may know if you are familiar with photography, black and white images are reversed with the black images on the mechanical showing clear on the negative film.

Figure 7-14. An X-Acto blade may be used to trim the edges.

This film is then re-shot, in order to produce a **printing plate.** When shot, the light only penetrates the clear areas, which represent the black images on the mechanical. These areas are the *only* ones which will contain ink on the final printed piece. *The actual color of the ink is irrelevant until the plate is made. If you wanted your ad to appear in all red, the process of assembling the mechanical would be exactly the same, except you would indicate in the margin of the mechanical the specific color you wished the piece to be printed in.*

If you wanted to print a piece that was more than one color, you would have to construct a separate mechanical for each color, each containing only those images, in their corresponding positions, to be printed in that color.

Figure 7-15. *Now, once everything is cut out, begin arranging it on the board, before cementing.*

If there is a full color illustration to be printed within your piece, then that illustration would have to be shot much like the photo would on a separate board.

If it seems rather complicated, a few simple applications of these instructions will quickly simplify it. Remember: keep all your original artwork and designs. Keep all type, illustrations and other elements stored away. If the first mechanical you work on takes a lot of time, or seems difficult, remember, the next will be much easier. If you keep all your images stored, you may find yourself using them again and again. Pretty soon, you'll be able to whip out your own ads in less than an hour! If you have any problems or other questions, your printer should be able to help you. One thing to remember: when you find a good printer, hang onto them. If they're helpful, show your appreciation, and keep coming back.

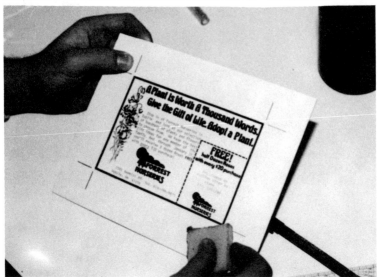

Figure 7-16. Now, your ad is ready to be sent to the publication.

Chapter
8

Advertising Agencies and How to Select Them

Up until this point, you have learned how you may develop your own personal advertising strategies without the use of an agency. But there comes a time when your budget and options expand so much that you may find it hard to get along without one.

When you've reached the point where you may want to expand your advertising expenditures, you have two options to get the most out of your money, of which you will be spending much. The first is to start your own **in-house agency**, by hiring your own advertising professionals full-time, or getting consultants part-time (the latter is rather expensive). Your business opens a department solely committed to advertising. In-house agencies may also work with full service ad agencies, with the separate agencies participating in only a portion of the overall campaign, thus only receiving a fraction of what they would if it were otherwise. More on these later.

The second option, and probably the better choice, if your business is rather small, is to turn to a full service advertising agency.

This chapter will tell you how agencies work. You may not find the knowledge immediately beneficial, but knowing how organizations and their businesses operate will give you a strong advantage when dealing with them.

A full-service agency handles everything. It covers market analysis, campaign and strategy planning, production, creative services (writing and art), and placing the ads. What specific services they personally do not handle under their own roof are hired out to other services or free-lancers by the agency itself, not the client.

The first steps an agency takes when beginning a new campaign (or deciding to accept one) are very similar to the ones you may have taken when utilizing the information given in the earliest chapters of this book. They ask the exact same questions about the marketability of your product or business and how to promote it.

How Ad Agencies Are Compensated

Advertising agencies receive compensation in three ways: commissions, fees and discounts from the media.

Many agencies will cover your advertising at no

additional cost to you, besides the charges for creativity (art and design), and the cost of placing the ad. The reason behind this is that the agency receives a 15 percent discount form the media, but they charge you the full amount. That 15 percent is their profit. If they don't consider you or your business to be worth much money, a smaller agency may charge you an added fee, or they won't give you the highest quality output.

If you do continue to handle all your advertising on your own, which includes correspondence, writing, planning and art (the writing and art may be hired out), you may call yourself an "in-house" agency (more on these later), therefore taking the 15 percent discount yourself. Check with the local media.

The traditional amount of commission for an agency is 15 percent. However, this does not include work on production, which includes creative work, like design, writing, and photography. You are charged a cost of these services (basically the ones which were summarized previously) plus an additional commission on top of that, which is runs between 17 and 18 percent.

Most agencies go on a commission basis, but this also depends on your business and potential for financial return. As stated earlier, they will charge you an additional fee, to insure a decent profit. From this point, you may negotiate with the agency to arrange a flat fee overall.

But any arrangement like this may put you at a disadvantage. Why? Suppose you are handling two accounts for two different clients. They are both trying to sell products, and one of the products has a much greater potential for yielding a hefty profit than the other. Of course, you would accept the job for this product on a commission basis, in which you will collect 15 percent of their profits. We'll call this client "Account A".

The other product does not show as much promise, so your enthusiasm for promoting it is not as high. But you accept the job anyway after negotiating it to a flat fee, which your client will pay upon completion of your share of the work. This client will be "Account B".

Which account do you think you will put your best efforts into, Account A or Account B?

You probably answered Account A. This does not indicate that you're dishonest. People in general work better at something when they see a direct and substantial profit (or benefit) resulting from those efforts. If they are being paid a flat rate, they'll get the same amount regardless of how much effort is put into it (to a degree of course). *The main concern with them is to get the job done on time.*

How Agencies Are Organized

Although different agencies vary slightly in how they are organized, it can be safely said that most of them have four different areas of responsibility: **(1) creativity; (2) marketing; (3) account services;** and **(4) management and finance.** Each of these areas have executives in charge of these departments, often titled **vice-presidents.**

(1) *Creative Services.* As indicated in the last two chapters, the effectiveness of the advertising campaign

depends largely on the results this department produces. The creative director decides how the public will see the client and his product. Although the basic message and who it is targeted to is decided in other departments, it is all in vain if the writers and artists of the creative department fail to translate the message into an attractive and convincing (not to mention eye-catching) advertisement.

The individual in charge is referred to as the **creative director.** This person must have a good acquaintance with both art and writing. Under him or her may be several other directors, in charge of either art or copywriting. Other directors may specialize in either print or broadcast media.

(2) *Marketing.* The responsibilities of this department are deciding what media to use, research (although this is often done through independent organizations), the approach to make the sale, and deciding who they want to sell to.

Each of these tasks is usually handled by mini-departments and the directors in charge of them. The media department not only selects the media, but also selects and buys the space and/or air time. The bigger the agency, the more divided the responsibilities (as in virtually any organization, regardless of department). A media buyer in a large agency may only handle a certain form of media, such as television. The research director will handle that task, or hire whoever does it on a freelance basis. The promotions director will have a staff which carefully analyzes and drafts out promotion strategies.

(3) *Account services.* This department handles

client/ agency relations. All elements of communication, which is crucial to the success of the campaign, goes through account services. This means presentation of ideas and storyboards, handling of finances, and, most importantly, understanding the needs and wants of the client. This cannot be done without the a fair knowledge of the client's business while also knowing the business of advertising.

The vice president of this department will usually, in larger agencies, hire account executives to head the account and the relationship with the client. This decision of who will be in charge of a particular account depends much on an individual's personal qualifications to suit the specific needs of the client.

(4) *Management and Finance.* Like any institution, ad agencies have administrative departments which handle the business side of the agency. This includes control of finances, employees, and office management.

Agency Networks

Since you will probably be dealing with a small to medium sized agency, you should know that many of these are joined in loose affiliations known as **agency networks.** Their function at first was similar to that of trade associations, helping each other in different areas of expertise. They even occasionally trade accounts with one another. Geographic dilemmas are often solved through networks as well. If all you want is to sell a product in a different city, much information about that city may not be known by your present agency, for obvious reasons. But if your agency belongs to the same network as another agency in that particular city, then you'll have the advantage.

Independent Services

As said before, although the full-service agency controls all aspects of the advertising campaign as far as the client is concerned, they will quite often hire out other agencies to perform specific tasks. These can range anywhere from free-lance artists to groups of creative people referring to themselves as **boutiques**. They are generally regarded as **independent creative services**. They handle the same responsibilities as the creative departments in agencies, but operate independently of them.

Media buying services evolved with the overall evolution of the media itself. The media today is a hundred times more complex than it was twenty years ago. People spend entire careers studying and analyzing the media and its effects on our culture. Many of these individuals whose professional concerns lie strictly with the media, and nothing else, find it more profitable to join together (although some may operate individually) and form these independent organizations. They not only choose the media and spots, but arrange for the purchasing of the spots.

In-house agencies, as stated before, are usually formed as departments of separate businesses. While some handle all elements of their own advertising, they will share responsibilities with full service agencies.

Most in-house agencies today operate with a small staff, and have most of the work competed through independent organizations. They oversee all the elements and bring them together, and then usually turn the final product over to a full service organization for placing. The standard 15 percent commission does not apply here. Usually fees are collected through a flat rate or a smaller commission. The overall goal of this is to save money, and is a prospect worth considering once enough advertising experience is gained, and a significant amount of future campaigns are planned.

What Is A Barter?

Have you ever watched a game show or variety show of some sort which involves filming in different locations throughout the world, such as *Lifestyles of the Rich & Famous* or *Mission: Impossible?* Ever notice at the end of these programs, there is always the shot of the airplane, with the words, "Transportation provided by Airlines in exchange for this announcement..."?

This is a form of **barter**, which is getting air time through exchange (more simply trade) of services or merchandise. No cash is involved whatsoever. It is quite often a money saver, depending on the circumstances. If you were a dealer in electronic equipment, the type that a TV or radio station might need, you may both save money by giving (or lending) some of your equipment to the station in exchange for air time. The expense of the equipment may be less than the price of the time, for you benefit, and the reverse for the station. When you do this, you are bartering out your merchandise.

Bartering is very common in sports. Do you think race car drivers have the top-of-the-line Goodyears because the driver bought them? Of course not. It's because he has the Goodyear logo stretched out along the front of his car, for everyone across the country who is watching the race to see.

Market Research Services

Like media research and analyzing, market research has become a highly complex and specialized field. Independent organizations which provide these services may be extremely valuable to agencies and their clients, especially if they are independent. Research conducted by the agency or the advertiser itself may yield biased results, decreasing the reliability of the information upon which the marketing strategy will be based.

There are many techniques of research, which rely on both technology and simple man power. Cable TV systems which are equipped with electronic feedback are extremely advantageous, as are mail-in questionnaires and phone surveys. Some are received more favorable than others. But a detailed account of the many forms of research would take many more pages than is allowed here.

Selecting An Agency

When choosing an agency, you must not do it hastily. For your situation, you will probably want to choose one in your city. A small to medium size agency may be your only choice, since the larger firms only deal with larger clients, on national campaigns.

Form a list of the potential agencies in your area. Visit them...let them know that you're in the market for selecting one. Don't allow yourself to be necessarily drawn toward the ones which may appear overly eager to serve you—remember: everyone is in business for himself.

Making the choice can be summarized by answering these questions:

(1) *How much experience does this agency have in my type of business?* If you run a home electronics store, have they advertised for other ones? If so, this can be good or bad. It's good if they aren't currently representing another business like yours. This means that they have the experience in your field (or perhaps not—the account executive may be long gone by now). Go to their former clients, and ask them what the agency was like, and how much did they help improve business.

It can be bad if they are still advertising for someone else, hence that other client is one of your competitors—in which case the agency probably wouldn't accept you anyway.

(2) *What kind of compensation will they expect?* When you started advertising, you had a very limited budget. By this time, we can assume that it has expanded somewhat. Understand that the best service merits the best compensation and you'll get ahead. Don't allow yourself to get too greedy.

(3) *What do I think of their other past campaigns?* The best way to judge an agency is to look at its portfolio. See the other campaigns, other than those related to yours. How diverse are they? How big is the range of clientele, in terms of types of businesses?

(4) *Do I feel comfortable with them?* The client/agency relationship is a long and ongoing process. If you don't like them or find it hard to communicate, it will be your money that's wasted, not theirs.

Knowing these simple fundamentals on advertising and the business should give you a great advantage when engaging in this challenging field.   Not everything may work the first time, but proper research and careful decisions provided by a wealth of feedback, will eventually pay off.

There is a great importance in learning to do things for yourself. This means making mistakes, and learning from them. Running your own business in this country is challenging, and most of the markets are highly competitive.   There is no one in the world of business you can trust totally...besides yourself. The fact that you are paying them means little.

Darwin wasn't the first to form the theory of evolution...he was the first to tell people about it.

About the author...

Keith F. Luscher is currently a publications and promotions director for a Columbus manufacturing and wholesale distributing company. His background stems not only in advertising and public relations, from the Journalism School at the Ohio State University, but also advertising and graphic design from the Columbus College of Art & Design. He has done work for organizations such as the United Way, as well as freelancing as an advertising copywriter and graphic designer. Many of his clients are small business operators.

I*ndex*

B

barter   122, 123
billboards   41
bleed poster   43
Book stocks   39, 40
boutiques   121
Boy's Life   6
brands   7, 10
broadcast   15, 18, 20
bus panel   41
business advertising   12
business cards   84
business magazines   16

C

car cards   46
catalogues   12, 40, 54
CBS   25
circulation   18, 26
classified advertising   51, 52, 53, 54, 83, 97
clip art   99
co-op mail advertising   38
co-ops   (see "cooperative advertising")
coding   58
cold press   88
commission   117
commissions   116, 117
"comp"   102, 103
competition   5
compiled lists   38
computers   97, 98
connotation   59
consumer advertising   12
consumer goods   2, 7
consumer magazines   16, 28, 30
consumer preferences   5
continuous–tone art   100